MW00893501

Mormonism:
A Latter Day Deception

Secret Ceremonials in Morman Temples

By

Martin Wishnatsky

P.O. Box 413
Fargo, ND 58107

goodmorals@linkup.net

XULON
PRESS

Mormonism: A Latter Day Deception
by Martin Wishnatsky

Printed in the United States of America

Library of Congress Control Number: 2003102349
ISBN 1-591604-94-X

All Scripture quotations are taken from the Authorized King James Version of the Bible.

Xulon Press
www.XulonPress.com

Xulon Press books are available in bookstores everywhere, and on the Web at www.XulonPress.com.

Introduction

The events and experiences recorded in this book took place between 1980 and 1982. Except for some excerpts offered on eBay in the year 2000, the manuscript has sat quietly in the closet for 20 years. Its relevance is as great now as it was then. The reason why the author was hesitant to publish it will be evident to the reader.

I hope it will be clear that I did not join the Mormon Church with the object of disclosing its secrets (little did I know there was anything to hide), but rather because I believed in it. The shock of the endowment ceremony in the Mormon Temple in Washington, D.C. determined me to research its history — with results that confirmed my forebodings.

To preserve the flow of the narrative, facts have been left as they were recorded in 1982, when the manuscript was written. Where subsequent events are of interest, a comment is added in brackets to set it off from the original text.

I express my appreciation to the Firestone Library at Princeton University for access to the stacks and manuscript sources.

Contents

PART ONE

The Washington Temple

In fact, there is nothing secret about the temple.
I have found nothing secret in or about our temples.
Apostle John A. Widtsoe
Utah Genealogical and Historical Magazine
April, 1921

I looked forward to my trip to the Mormon Temple in Washington, D.C. with great anticipation at the opportunity of learning sublime truths and participating in a solemn and holy ceremony of worship. "You can expect to enjoy one of the wonderful experiences of your life in the house of the Lord," read an article in the Church magazine on temples. "A beautiful and meaningful experience" was promised. I anticipated "clothing my mind in purity of thought" and "receiving instruction from the Spirit." The Temple ceremonial is called "the endowment." As Elder Elray Christiansen explained: "To endow is to enrich, to give to another something long-lasting and of much worth." I was promised also "power from God," spiritual power as in the biblical "endowed with power from on high." I was told also to antici-pate receiving an education "relative to the Lord's purposes and plans." As a believer in the mission of the Church of Jesus Christ of Latter-day Saints, I welcomed the following statement: "Participation in temple work provides dynamic, vivid useful instruction in gospel principles, and the temple is a place for contemplation and prayer. The temple is a sanctuary from the world, a bit of heaven on earth...."

I appreciated the fact that to a believer certain information could have an impact impossible for a non-believer, that just as an advanced course in engineering could be appreciated only by those trained in the fundamentals of the discipline, so an under-standing of the rarer truths of heaven required first a faithful adherence to certain basic tenets. Therefore, Elder Mark E. Petersen seemed to make sense when he explained: "The holy ordinances were never fully made known to the world at large; they were too sacred, but the chosen and faithful participate in all solemnity."

As I disposed my mind for my first visit to what the *Washington Post* called "the mysterious citadel on the Beltway," I studied Elder John A. Widtsoe's article "Looking toward the Temple." He spoke of certain "ceremonies pertaining to godli-ness." "The simple ceremonies help us to go out from the temple with the high resolve to lead lives worthy of the gifts of the gospel." Did I have any problems that were bothering me? Rest assured, said Elder Widtsoe, himself an Apostle and one of the foremost theologians of the Church, "every person who enters this sacred place in faith and prayer will find help in the solution of life's problems."

"Gratitude for this privilege," I read, "and an eager desire to possess the spirit of the occasion should overflow in our hearts." Here would be distilled and presented the essence of the restored gospel: "Indeed, in the temple the whole gospel is epitomized." So profound were the truths presented that "it is not to be expected that the temple ceremonies can be comprehended in full detail the first time...." The promises and assurances continued to flow:

> It is spiritual fitness and understanding that one receives in the temple.
>
> From beginning to end, going through the temple is a glorious experience. It is uplifting, informative. It gives courage.
>
> The laws of the temple and the covenants of the endowment are beautiful, helpful, simple, and easily understood. To observe them is equally simple.

Culminating this overture of promise, Elder Widtsoe concluded that "all history seems to revolve about the building and use of temples." The temple, I thought, would be a grander and more inspiring worship service — finer music, more sublime; longer, more learned and more revealing discourses.

Temple Recommend Interview

At my initial interview for a Temple Recommend, the Bishop moved quickly through the prescribed list of questions, all of which I had expected, except the question: "Have you been wearing your Temple garments?" "Have I what?" I thought. But before I could say anything, he said: "Oh, that doesn't apply to you," and moved on to the next question. During the week, a little puzzled at this, I asked a Mormon friend to elucidate. "You'll find out about that in the Temple," he said. "The garments are the same as the ones that Adam and Eve wore in the Garden of Eden; they're for protection." At my final Temple Recommend interview with the Stake president, he asked me if I knew about the garments. He told me I could purchase them at the Temple, and that I must wear them continually, day and night. By way of explanation he said that he had just bought a number of new sets of underwear before he went through the Temple for the first time and afterwards had to throw them all away.

"Is this where it gets weird?" I asked a friend when I heard about church-issue underwear, but, in fact, I had no serious qualms — mostly eager anticipation. I knew there would be some ceremonies, and I had been told vaguely about "making covenants with the Lord," but still in my mind I envisioned a solemn and moving religious service. "Do you know the new name the faithful receive from Jesus?" a friend asked me. "It's mentioned in the Book of Revelation. Well, you'll find out your new name at the temple."

Preliminaries

Most of the people in our temple trip had their own temple garments. Since I was new, I had to rent mine for eight dollars at the garment desk, which looked like a Hollywood version of heaven's clothing dispensary — beatifically-smiling white-clad matrons issuing packets of freshly laundered celestial garments. I went with the men to the men's locker room where we shed our civvies and put on temple whites. Since I was "doing my own endowment," I had first to dress semi-nude, covered only by a "shield" — a square piece of white cloth with a circle cut in the center to fit over your head. I then proceeded to "washing and anointing."

Two attendants with ecstatic expressions dripped some water on my head and blessed the various parts of my body. This first coat of blessings was repeated and "sealed" with drops of consecrated oil. "Your new name," one of the blessors whispered to me, "which will be your name through all eternity, is Enoch."

I emerged enameled with blessings and quite ecstatic myself. As I left the blessing area, I accidentally overheard another initiate receiving his washing and anointing. "Your new name, which will be your name through all eternity," I heard the attendant say to him, "is Enoch."

Returning to the locker room, I discarded the shield, put on a white jump suit and hospital slippers, placed a packet of unknown content under my arm, and padded down the hall for a briefing on the "endowment." The speaker wore a white suit, white shirt, white tie, white shoes and white socks. He impressed upon us the solemnity and sacredness of the endowment and offered us the opportunity to back out. If we went ahead, we must be willing to "keep the covenants of the Lord." No one demurred and we filed down the hall to the endowment room where the others were waiting for us.

The Endowment Room

The endowment room reminded me of a Hollywood screening room. To my amazement, no sooner had we been seated — under the stiff gaze of solemn-visaged ushers in white — than the lights dimmed and a movie began. Elohim, Jesus and Michael appeared in Technicolor holding a meeting amidst the porticos of Heaven. "Look," said one, "there is matter unorganized. Let us go down and organize it and make an earth to dwell upon." "It is good," said Elohim. The first day, the second day, the third day ... scenes of seas roaring, birds chirping, etc. passed before us. Jesus and Michael reported back to Elohim after each day's work. "It is good," said Elohim. Adam was created, blond and Nordic — and his wife the same. "It is good," said Elohim, sporting a Santa Claus beard. The devil now appeared and lured Eve into eating the forbidden fruit. Adam partook out of pity for Eve, and they were driven out of Eden into "the lone and dreary world." But, lo, here came

Peter (an actor on WKRP in Cincinnati), James, and John with a message of redemption. Peter shooed the devil away and then shook Adam's hand with a knowing look in his eye.

The movie faded; the lights came up. Before the screen stood a low altar covered in white lace. A Book of Mormon and a Bible sat on top of it. Behind the altar stood a man in white with a grave countenance. "Open your packets," he said, "and put on your robes." I took out a pleated white robe and draped it over myself. Someone helped me tie it at the shoulder to keep it from slipping off. Next came a puffy white hat. "Put on your aprons," said the leader. Out came a green silk apron with fig leaves embroidered on it. I tied it around my waist. "I sure hope this gets better," I said to myself, "because it can't get much worse."

Oaths and Grips

"We will now administer the first grip of the Aaronic priesthood," said the leader. "Please rise. We wish all to receive it." After a demonstration in front of the room, the attendants walked up and down the rows giving everyone the special handshake. "We will now administer the oath," said the man in white, "with its accompanying sign and penalty." The sign he demonstrated by drawing his finger across his throat. I stared in amazement. "Repeat the oath after me," he said, "while simultaneously making the sign." The oath is: "I would rather suffer my life to be taken than to reveal the first grip of the Aaronic priesthood." The attendants carefully watched to see that everyone complied with the instructions.

Dressed as I was in the most absurd costume I have ever worn — a pleated white robe over a white jump suit, adorned with a green silk apron embroidered with fig leaves and topped off with a puffy pleated chef's cap complete with tassel — and surrounded as I was by ardent believers and steely-eyed spotters, I deemed it

prudent not to draw attention to myself by any gesture of disbe-
lief, dismay or regret. I had come to Washington in a motor home
with other Mormons from my ward and would have to go back
with them. Given the nature of the oaths that were being administered, I decided not to make an issue of anything. A wise man,
even if he finds out that he has made a mistake, does not stand up
in a moving roller coaster and try to get off. He holds on, grits his
teeth, and waits till the journey is completed before disembarking.

"Be seated," said the leader. The lights dimmed and the movie
resumed. More trials of Adam and Eve. The lights came up again,
a new handshake was demonstrated, and an oath, sign and penalty
administered. The sign was obscure to me, but required some
hand motion in the area of the chest. More movie followed and we
rose for the administration of a third grip. The sign this time
looked as if one were unzipping his belly. The penalty as before
was the same: "I would rather suffer my life to be taken…" we all
chanted in unison. "This had better be leading somewhere," I
thought to myself, "because I've about had it." A fourth handshake followed. For the record, I include a description of the four
secret grips.

Grip One. In the first handshake of Mormonism one grips the
hand of the other person in the usual fashion and presses his thumb
upon the knuckle of the index finger of the other person. This is the
first grip of the Aaronic priesthood. The Sign is the finger across
the throat. The penalty for revealing the grip is your life.

Grip Two. In the second handshake of Mormonism, one
presses the thumb in between the knuckle of the index finger and
the knuckle of the middle finger. The sign is a motion in the area of
the chest. The penalty is your life, should you reveal it.

Grip Three. In the third handshake, one presses his thumb
against the middle of the palm of the other person and at the same
time extends his forefinger along the back of the other person's

hand, pressing thumb and forefinger together to indicate the location of the stigmata of Christ in the palm. This is the first grip of the Melchizedek priesthood. The sign is drawing the hand across the gut. The penalty, again, is your life.

Grip Four. In the fourth handshake, known as the Patriarchal Grip, one interlocks pinkies with the other person and at the same time extends the forefinger to press against the wrist of the other person. Known as the Sure Sign of the Nail, this grip symbolizes the nail that supposedly was driven through the wrist of the crucified when the original nail tore out of His Palm. At a Mormon Temple marriage ceremony, the couple kneel at an altar, join hands across it in the Patriarchal Grip, and are thus "sealed" together.

At the Veil

Instead of an oath and penalty to accompany the Patriarchal Grip, which is the second handshake of the Melchizedek priesthood, the movie screen lifted — to reveal a polyester curtain with strange markings on it shaped like "V's" and square "L's". I could vaguely make out men standing at intervals behind the curtain. Various attendants, male and female, stood in front of it, dressed in Temple white and smiling broadly at us. "What now?" I thought, and imagined a tattooing or a bloodletting as a fit culmination for the ghoulish experience that had so far transpired in the endowment room. But, no. The curtain was no more than the "veil" that separates this world from the next. Having, like Adam, been "true and faithful" in receiving the four grips, taking the oaths of secrecy and agreeing to the penalties, we now qualified to pass into the celestial kingdom. The men behind the curtain were representations of Elohim, waiting to welcome us into bliss. First, however, we had to recite the grips and oaths correctly. The "V's" and "L's" were openings in the curtain to allow the Elohims to put their hands through to test us. The attendants were there as prompters in case we had forgotten anything.

An attendant led me to the veil. He lifted a tiny hammer suspended from a bracket and rapped "tink-tink-tink" to let Elohim know that he had a visitor. After reviewing the handshakes with me, Elohim taught me an elaborate blessing while engaging me through the curtain in a full-body hug on the "five points of fellowship" — foot to foot, knee to knee, chest to chest, cheek to cheek, and mouth to ear. A gentle chorus of tink-tinks filled the room mingling with the murmur of endowees reciting their litanies and the muffled tones of the clones of God uttering their blessings through the curtain. At last my own Elohim released me, parted the veil, and, taking my hand, pulled me behind the curtain. When I looked puzzled as to what celestial revelation might come next as the culmination and perhaps compensation for what had so far transpired, he gestured for me to walk on.

The Celestial Room

I did so and came into the "Celestial Room," a Louis XIV-style lobby with a beautiful chandelier, ornate stuffed furniture and lush carpeting. Other endowees were present, sitting quietly or whispering softly and reverently to one another. "I guess we wait here," I thought, "for the real pay-off. I sure hope it gets better." "How did you like it?" one of my Mormon friends asked. And it hit me. This is it; it's over. Looking at my stricken face, another friend said, "Whatever you may think, Martin, I want you to know that God is very pleased with what you've done today." We then went downstairs and ate lunch.

Endowing the Departed

After lunch (I hardly said a word), we came back upstairs and I was given a name typed on a slip of paper which I pinned to my jumpsuit. Having been endowed myself, I could now do endowments "for the dead." I was to stand in for a Matthew Ramage who had died in 1856. Since no soul can enter the Celestial Kingdom without an endowment, the Church, as the sole custodian of this ceremony, feels obligated to perform endowments for every soul who ever lived. Only in this way can those who died before Christ restored the true gospel to Joseph Smith in 1829 ever have a hope of full salvation. By standing in for Matthew Ramage, I was performing a small part of this holy work. First stop was the "New Name Room," where an attendant whispered Matthew Ramage's "new name" to me. "Your new name, which will be your name through all eternity," he said, "is Enoch." We proceeded to the Endowment Room. The same ceremony as before took place replete with movie, oaths, gestures, penalties and robes. "When you take the oaths," instructed the leader, "think of the name of your proxy as if you are that person." A small English graveyard was endowed in this session, a few of the stand-ins nodding off occasionally — perhaps to the eternal detriment of those for whom they stood as proxy. "Jesus was a proxy for us on the cross; it's the least we can do," said one Mormon.

Having endowed both myself and Matthew Ramage, leaving both of us in a position to give the proper handshakes at heaven's gate, I felt I had done a full day's work and declined the opportunity to go through a third time. The movie was beginning to wear on me. "Heaven has enough Enoch's for one day," I said to myself.

The End

After changing back into street dress and stuffing my used garments into the laundry chute, a Mormon couple took me to the Garment Center in the basement of the Temple where I purchased four sets of sacred underwear. They were embroidered with an "L" over the left breast, a "V" over the right, and a straight line across the left knee as a reminder that every knee shall bow to Christ. I slung the bag under my arm, stopped to have my picture taken in front of the Temple, and rode home in silent consternation.

PART TWO

The Princeton Stacks

No jot, iota, or tittle of the temple rites
is otherwise than uplifting or sanctifying.
Apostle James E. Talmage
The House of the Lord
1912

The conveying of secret handshakes sealed by an oath of secrecy on penalty of death seemed a ludicrous and chilling culmination to my quest for divine truth. No pure and holy being could wish such a form of worship, I felt, and thereafter began to spend one day a week doing research on Mormon history at Princeton University's Firestone Library.

That the Mormons took seriously the absurdities of the Temple became evident upon reading an address by Elder Theodore M. Burton, Assistant to the Twelve Apostles, delivered to the October, 1968 General Conference in the Salt Lake Tabernacle.

My dear brothers and sisters, and all who are watching and listening to these messages: If you were to approach a military installation some dark night, you would be immediately challenged by a sentry with the question, "Who goes there?" If you were to answer that challenge with the word "friend," the sentry would answer, "Advance, friend, and give the password." If you were neither able to give the password nor to identify yourself, you would be placed in an embarrassing and dangerous position.

Yet millions of those presently living on the earth are totally unprepared for death and to enter through the gates of the celestial kingdom. They know neither the password nor will they be able to identify themselves as a son or a daughter of God.

Despite Elder Burton's admonition, I could not believe that heaven was organized as the Mormons asserted. Rather, I asked myself, where on earth did Joseph Smith acquire these ceremonies?

The Masonic Connection

On the way home from the Washington Temple, a Church member mentioned that the Mormon Temple ceremony shared some similarities with Masonic rituals. Masonry, he explained to me, was a corrupted form of the true Temple worship established by Solomon and reinstated in its original purity by Christ's revelation to Joseph Smith. I began by looking up "Masonry" in the card catalogue. The Masons, I discovered, were a secret society bound together by peculiar handshakes sealed by oaths and blood penalties! Each Masonic "degree" has its own special grip, oath and penalty.

Entered Apprentice. A new Mason is known as an "Entered Apprentice." The Entered Apprentice's penalty for disclosing his secret grip is to have "the throat cut across from ear to ear, the tongue torn out by the roots, and the body buried up to the neck below the high tide line." The initiate is required to take an oath agreeing to suffer this penalty should he ever convey the secret handshake to anyone not bound by the same oath.

Fellow Craft. The Entered Apprentice, having proved true and faithful to the Order, is then qualified to advance and become a "Fellow Craft." The Fellow Craft learns a special handshake to commemorate his promotion. He takes an oath of secrecy confirmed with a penalty of having "the left breast torn open and the heart and lungs ripped out." "This is probably what that hand motion in the area of the chest represented," I thought.

"So I agreed to have my heart ripped out, did I, if I ever told anyone about this nonsense?" My feeling of lighthearted spoofing evaporated when I read the following account of what happened to a disillusioned Mason who told tales. Reports Samuel G. Anderton (March 15, 1830):

> While struggling on the floor, they cut his throat! And then his left side and breast open, so as to show his heart!! Some, very few Masons present, seemed by their looks, to express some sympathy and compassion: while the rest, using the most profane, revengeful language, with their fists clenched, grinned with horrid approbation.

"The next day," continues Anderton, a sailor, "after we got to sea, I threw my apron and masonic papers overboard." Apron?

"God help me!" I said to myself, and read on.

Master Mason. The next level after a Fellow Craft is to become a "Master Mason." Failure to conceal the secret grips of a Master Mason calls for "quartering the body and burning the bowels to ash." "This must be related to the unzipping of the belly," I thought.

Royal Arch Mason. Finally, I read of the penalty attending the next level of Masonic advancement, that of a "Royal Arch Mason." Such an exalted individual, should he fall from grace, must submit to be scalped and his "brains scorched by the sun," a punishment likely to deter all except the most devoted sun worshipper.

The Parallels

Clearly the Mormons and the Masons were branches of the same tree. The Mormons slit the throat; so did the Masons. The Masons tore out the heart, which seemed to correspond with the sign of the second grip of the Aaronic priesthood. The Masons took an oath of disembowelment, which seemed to parallel the belly sign administered in the Temple. The Masons wore aprons; the Mormons wore aprons. In addition, I later observed, Masonic temples looked a lot like the original Mormon temples. Who came first? No question about that.

The Mormon Church was founded in 1829; the first Mormon temple was built in 1836, and the first endowments given in the 1840's in Nauvoo, Illinois. The Masons went back a long way. Mozart was a Mason; George Washington, too. "Did Joseph Smith," I asked, "have any knowledge of the Masons?"

Joseph Smith and Masonry

The details of the Masonic rituals were first published in 1826 by a disaffected Mason named William Morgan. At the time his book was in press, Morgan was kidnapped and murdered. His death prompted a tremendous outcry against secret societies that became an important strand in New York politics.

Morgan lived in western New York, only a few miles from the residence of the Smith family. Joseph's older brother, Hyrum, was a Mason at the time of Morgan's abduction and murder and may have been familiar with the members of the lodges that carried out the deed. In 1842, Joseph Smith established a Masonic lodge in Nauvoo and on the first night of his participation in the Order received the unprecedented honor of being raised from Entered Apprentice directly through Fellow Craft to Master Mason, experiencing the whole panoply of oaths and gruesome penalties. Less than two months later he initiated his followers into the "newly revealed" Mormon temple mysteries.

The Smith brothers did not need to learn about Masonry from anyone else. They knew the oaths and penalties at first hand, for they were Masons themselves.

The Original Endowment

In the original endowment ceremony Joseph Smith employed unchanged the gruesome Masonic language to describe the penalties. The phrase: "I would rather suffer my life to be taken" is a twentieth century alteration and softening of the original Mormon endowment oaths. Professor Walter Wolfe, formerly of the Brigham Young College faculty at Logan, Utah, testified before the U.S. Senate Committee on Privileges and Elections on February 7, 1906, relating a verbatim and gesture-by-gesture account of the endowment ceremony of that time. Instead of saying "I would rather suffer my life to be taken..." while drawing the finger across the throat, the Mormons of 1906 said: "I agree that my throat may be cut from ear to ear, and my tongue torn out by the roots." I can only imagine what I would have done, had the leader thrown these words at us in the endowment room. Undoubtedly I would have fled or been led away in a state of catatonic paralysis long before I could have embraced Elohim at the "veil."

My guess is that as the Church expanded its missionary efforts after World War I and began to attract a steady flow of convert members from urban America, the periodic uproar in the endowment rooms caused by the administering of these oaths to people who had no family roots in the Church was sufficient to inspire a revelation from Elohim that led to the abandonment of the offending language.

That strange sign in the chest area, testified Professor Wolfe, "is made by extending the right hand across the left breast, directly over the heart; then drawing it rapidly from left to right, with the elbow at the square; then dropping the hand by the side." The original oath that accompanied this sign was more than sufficient to explain its import. The penalty for violating the secrecy of the second grip of the Aaronic priesthood, records Professor Wolfe, is "that our breasts may be torn out and given to the birds of the air and the beasts of the field." Surely such a penalty was reasonable for violating an oath taken before God. If a mere Fellow Craft could abide such a penalty, why not a Latter-Day Saint?

The sign that I remembered only as a gesture somewhat like unzipping the belly is described in detail by Professor Wolfe: "In this, the left hand is placed palm upright, directly in front of the body, there being a right angle formed at the elbow; the right hand, palm down, is placed under the elbow of the left; then drawn sharply across the bowels, and both hands are dropped at the side." The significance of this gesture, the hardest of all to learn (we were rehearsed several times as a group before the actual formal oath-taking), became clear upon reading the original penalty. Should the secret of the third grip be revealed, "you agree that your body may be cut asunder and all your bowels gush out." Now there's a man's oath, a far cry from the namby-pamby "I would rather suffer my life to be taken…" of modern time.

Mormonism: A Christian Takeoff on Masonry

Mormonism is a marriage of revival Christianity and Masonic ritual, a blood cult with a Christian face. Elohim's embrace through the curtain on the "five points of fellowship" is straight out of Masonry as are the "V's" and "L's" cut into the "veil" and sewn into the garments. The "L" is the Masonic tri-square and the "V" the compass. No doubt remained that Joseph Smith had stolen the Mormon Temple rituals from the Masons and worked them into a playlet about Adam and Eve.

Sitting on a chair in C-level of the Princeton stacks, I leaned back and took it all in. To find out about the Mormons, I had to find out about the Masons. To uncover one truth, I had to probe into an even more disturbing reality. The Mormons, a tightly-knit civilization within a civilization, are mostly considered to be in a world of their own. The Masons, however, are perhaps the largest fraternal order in the western world. Hundreds of thousands, indeed millions, of successful business and professional men are Masons, including former President Gerald Ford. What kind of a world is this, I wondered, in which the most intimate of fraternal and even religious associations are sealed by secret obligations of murder?

History of the Sacred Underwear

Setting these disturbing contemplations aside, I completed my examination of the day's events at the Temple by dredging out some information on the history of the religious underwear I was now obligated to wear. Originally, I discovered, the garment, embroidered with square and compass, was long-sleeved and extended to the ankles. Joseph Smith introduced it "by revelation" at the same time he began the temple ceremonial. Fitting around the neck like a T-shirt, it compelled women to wear high-necked long-sleeved dresses that extended to the ankles. Not everyone liked this, prompting a speech by Joseph F. Smith, a son of Joseph Smith's brother Hyrum, who became prophet of the Church in 1901.

> The Lord has given us garments of the Holy Priesthood, and you know what that means. And yet there are those of us who mutilate them, in order that we may follow the foolish, vain and (permit me to say) indecent practices of the world. In order that such people will imitate the fashions, they will not hesitate to mutilate that which should be held by them the most sacred of all things in the world, next to their own virtue, next to their own purity of life. They should hold these things that God has given unto them sacred unchanged and unaltered from the very pattern which God gave them. Let us have the moral courage to stand against the opinions of fashion, and especially when fashion compels us to break a covenant and so commit a grievous sin.
>
> *Improvement Era,* 9:813-14.

Nonetheless, when the endowment oaths were modified from their primitive starkness to what they are today, the garments also were abbreviated. The bulky item that extended from neck to ankle gave way to a short-sleeved style that ended just below the knee. Originally all in one piece, today's cotton armor comes in a one-piece and a two-piece fashion. Many old-timers blanched at what they considered "mutilation" of a sacred article of clothing revealed personally to Joseph Smith by Jesus Christ. Mystic powers of protection are ascribed to the garments. According to one popular story, a man emerged alive from a blazing auto wreck because the flames had been unable to burn any flesh protected by the garments. Some say that Joseph Smith was shot and killed in Carthage jail in 1844 because he was not wearing his garments that day.

In the nineteenth century the knee mark was cut into the garment with a knife during the endowment. The cut occasionally slashed the flesh of the endowee, prompting an eventual outcry from the scarred participants that halted the procedure.

No Mormon can attend the Temple (Temple recommends are subject to yearly renewal) unless he faithfully wears his garments "continually" — waking and sleeping. Heber C. Kimball, second only to Brigham Young in the early days in Utah, said in his Celestial Room discourses that for safety's sake he never completely took off one garment before putting on a fresh one, but would put one leg into the new garment while the old one still dangled around his other leg. New endowees are instructed not to show the garments to a non-initiate lest they be held up to ridicule. One Mormon housewife explained that when she hung them on the line to dry, she put a row of sheets on either side to conceal them from view. Worn-out garments are to be burned or cut up with scissors. Faithful Mormons are buried in their garments and the Temple robes as well. An exposé of the endowment ceremony that appeared in the *Salt Lake Tribune* many years before Professor Wolfe's description to the U.S. Senate, contains the following explanation:

> Before I go further I must tell how they believe the entrance into heaven is to be gained on the morning of the resurrection. Peter will call up the men and the

women.... If the marks on the garments are found to correspond with those on the veil (the dead are buried in the whole paraphernalia), if you can give the grips and tokens, and your new name, and you are dressed properly in your robes, why, then, one has a sure permit to heaven, and will pass by the angels ... to a more exalted glory....

Concluding Thoughts

The Veteran's Administration today has three standard insignia that may be engraved upon tombstones of departed veterans: the cross, the star of David, and the angel Moroni (a Book of Mormon character). Perhaps the Mormon representatives in Congress can request that the graves of the Founding Fathers, who died before the blessed garments were restored to earth, be opened and Temple garments laid upon the bones, that the authors of the Declaration of Independence and the Constitution not be found to lack "wedding garments" and be excluded from the celestial feast on the Day of Resurrection.

And, doubtlessly, some day soon, if it has not already occurred, their descendants and all the rest of those who ever lived will be baptized and endowed by proxy in a Mormon temple — that the followers of Joseph Smith may be the saviors of mankind and the rapidly expanding galaxy of Mormon temples may resound with the "tink-tinks" of celestial hammers opening the portals of heaven to all mankind.

PART THREE

Holy Murder

We would not kill a man, of course,
unless we killed him to save him.
Brigham Young
1855

Having satisfied myself as to the character and origin of the Temple ceremonies, I knew I could no longer be a Mormon. Nevertheless, I felt quite uneasy at actually leaving the Church and, especially, telling them why I was leaving.

First Sunday after the Temple Visit

The Sunday morning after our trip to the Temple the Bishop's First Counselor, as militant a Mormon as you will find, called me to the stand to testify of my experience. I'm sure he wanted to see if they were going to have any trouble with me and put me on the spot to find out. If I told these people what I actually thought ("I have now found out that this institution is actually evil…."), would my life be in danger? The idea was too fantastic to credit, but, taking no chances, I talked around the subject ("It's hard to talk about something you're not supposed to talk about ... ha, ha, ha...."), giving no hint of my true feelings. Who knew what these people were capable of? I didn't feel like finding out.

Discreet Departure

Several weeks later I told the Bishop that I was moving out of the area and that I would no longer be around. I said my good-byes, gave my farewell speech ("Thank you for all the love you've shown me"), and departed from the Church. As far as anyone knew, I was still a good Mormon. But in my heart Brother Wishnatsky was dead.

Keep Silent or Speak Out?

What business is it of mine, I reasoned, to expose the strange religious customs of these people? I've walked away, and that's that. What a relief! My life is my own again. On the other hand, I asked, was it fair for the Mormons to recruit people into a religion and then suddenly bind them with blood covenants? The bait was salvation, but the hook was death and the fear of death.

Didn't I have a moral obligation to say something about these tactics? Thirty thousand full-time missionaries are in the streets pulling in 200,000 converts a year. Yet no one has an idea of what the score really is until he gets into the Endowment Room — and then it's too late. The Federal Trade Commission regulates commerce to protect the consumer against commercial predators. The Food and Drug Administration regulates the drug industry and food production. The Securities and Exchange Commission regulates the brokerage houses and the Federal Aviation Administration the airlines. The Interstate Commerce Commission regulates interstate commerce; the Federal Communications Commission the airwaves and the Nuclear Regulatory Commission nuclear power — all to protect the public against those who would utilize economic power unfairly. On top of these administrative protections lie the product liability laws interpreted by the courts, all to shield us against those who would take our money and give us nothing in return.

What about those who would take our souls and give only terror in return? Shouldn't there be a truth-in-packaging law for them, too? Even suspected criminals are read their rights. What about the guileless soul, who perhaps has suffered a loss of hope, and is vulnerable to the salvation sellers? Doesn't he deserve a little pamphlet of disclosure from the missionaries along with the propaganda and the carefully-rehearsed speeches? Doesn't he have any recourse to get his tithing back when he discovers, with no forewarning, that he is in a death cult?

Perhaps, however, I thought, religion is not a fit subject for government regulation. In that case I felt personally obligated to publish the truth myself. On the one hand, I felt that Mormonism was no more to be taken seriously than a religious spoof on Saturday Night Live. It seemed to me a farce concocted by a salvation-minded P.T. Barnum. On the other hand, these people seemed very serious, and there were five million of them. They say the Mafia only kills its own and those who have made deals with them. Well, I was one of them, fully inducted and endowed. And it is hard to imagine that a Mafioso is bound under oaths any more strict than I had taken. I could shuffle backwards, grinning and bowing, and just fade away, my lips sealed tightly. Surely there were many who ended up this way. But if I published the truth about the pool of blood at the end of the Mormon rainbow, would I actually be endangering my own life, fantastic as that thought seemed?

Should I think twice before telling anyone that I could no longer be a Mormon — and explaining exactly why? I drove back to

Princeton, dug into the records of nineteenth-century American history and discovered that the answer was "yes."

Holy Murder

Numerous firsthand accounts of the early days of Mormonism amply documented the truth that "holy murder" had indeed been practiced by the Church of Jesus Christ of Latter-day Saints. These executions, carried out by a private police force known as the "High Police," took various forms in keeping with the temple oaths. Slitting the throat is the one most commonly mentioned. Presumably once this one has been inflicted, the others are no longer necessary. These ceremonial killings were described euphemistically as "saving" the victim, as in "Where is so and so? We haven't seen him lately." "Oh, didn't you hear? He got 'saved' the other night." "Fed him to the catfish" had its place as did the phrases "used him up," "slipped his breath," "put him out of the way," and "sent him over the rim." After the migration to Utah, the term "salt him down in the lake" came into vogue.

Just as the French have a great variety of terms for describing foods that are lacking in English, the early Mormons had many words for murder, reflecting their peculiar involvement with this craft. Invoking vengeance on the disloyal was known as "praying for our enemies." Killing them secretly was known as "not letting the right hand know what the left hand is doing."

Joseph Smith taught his followers that to kill those who violated their covenants was praiseworthy in the eyes of God. The first endowment ceremony, he explained, took place on the Mount of Transfiguration, where Christ instructed Peter, James and John in the secret handshakes and then bound them with oaths of blood should they ever forsake their loyalty to Him. This doctrine appears frequently in Church writings, and is cited in the work *Doctrines of Salvation* written by Joseph Fielding Smith,

Prophet of the Church in the years 1970-72. After coming down from the Mount of Transfiguration, the Apostles bound the other members of the twelve to loyalty on penalty of death as well. When Judas betrayed Christ, they killed him in fulfillment of their endowment oaths. An eyewitness reports that Joseph Smith "talked of dissenters and cited us to the case of Judas, saying that Peter told him in a conversation a few days ago that he himself hung Judas for betraying Christ...." *The Reed Peck Manuscript* (1839).

The "Salt" Sermon

Anyone who has attended a Sunday morning service in a neighborhood Mormon chapel will recall the presiding officer, the bishop or one of his counselors, announcing the names of members who were being "called" to new positions or "released" from old ones. In each case it is requested that the congregation "signify by the usual sign" their assent to the changes. The sign given is the raising of the right hand. For those who have been through the Temple, the right hand is raised "to the square," for this is the position in which it is held when making covenants of blood in the Temple. In the early days of Mormonism, such a ceremony often indicated that the death squad was about to march. In 1838, for instance, when the Mormons were contending for the country around Independence, Missouri, Sidney Rigdon — Joseph Smith's second-in-command — held a meeting. "Mr. Rigdon then commenced making covenants with uplifted hands," wrote one eyewitness. "The first was that if any man attempted to move out of the country," anyone noticing this action "should kill him and haul him aside into the brush." In what became known as the "Salt Sermon," Rigdon declared that "the church was the salt, that dissenters were the salt that had lost its savor, and that they were literally to be trodden under the feet of the church until their bowels should be gushed out. He referred to the case of Judas, informing the people that he did not fall headlong and his bowels gush out without assistance, but that the apostles threw him, and with their feet trampled them out! He also said that Ananias and Sapphira, his wife, did not fall down dead as translated but that Peter and John slew them, and the young men, or deacons, carried them out and buried them." William Harris, *Mormonism Portrayed* (1841).

The idea that Christ taught His apostles to kill His enemies continued in the Church after Joseph Smith's death in 1844. In a Sunday sermon given in Salt Lake City in the late 1850's, Heber C. Kimball, grandfather of the current Mormon prophet, explained again that the apostles killed Judas in keeping with their endowment oaths. "It is said in the Bible," related Kimball, "that Judas' bowels gushed out, but they actually kicked him until his bowels came out." He declared his determination to enforce in Utah the same penalties that Peter and John had inflicted in Jerusalem. "I know the day is right at hand," he said, "when men will forfeit their priesthood and turn against us and against the covenants they have made, and they will be destroyed as Judas was." *Journal of Discourses* 6:125-126.

Kill Thy Enemies

The traditional Christian doctrine of "love thy enemies" in Mormon hands after passing through the blood rituals became "kill thy enemies." In Missouri in the 1830's, wrote Benjamin F. Johnson, a friend of Joseph Smith, "we were taught to 'pray for our enemies' that God would damn them and give us power to kill them." The first Mormon temple service ever in Kirtland, Ohio in 1836 turned into a spectacular cursing session. "They spent the day in fasting and prayer," records William Harris. "The fast was broken by eating light wheat bread, and drinking as much wine as they saw proper, ... Smith ... telling them that the wine was consecrated and would not make them drunk." Mormon elder George A. Smith, also present at the dedication, relates: "After the people had fasted all day, they sent out and got wine and bread....They ate and drank and prophesied until some of the High Council of Missouri stepped into the stand, and, as righteous Noah did when he awoke from his wine, commenced to curse their enemies." *Journal of Discourses* 2:216. Heber C. Kimball continued the cursing tradition out in Utah. "Will the president that sits in the chair of state be tipped from his seat?" he asked a Sunday congregation. "Yes, he will die an untimely death, and God Almighty will curse him.... I curse them in the name of the Lord Jesus Christ...." *Journal of Discourses* 5:133.

That the death orders came right from the top and that the practice originated with Joseph Smith is well documented. "I have heard the Prophet say," recorded Thomas B. Marsh, "that he would yet tread down his enemies and walk over their dead bodies." (Affidavit, Richmond, Mo., October 24, 1838) One of the original Mormons, John Whitmer, in his memoir of the Church records the following incident: "Smith called a council of the leaders together in which he stated that any person who said a word against the heads of the church should be driven over these prairies as a chased deer by a pack of hounds." John D. Lee, a member of Joseph Smith's bodyguard, reports:

> I knew of many men being killed in Nauvoo by the Danites (the assassination squad). It was then the rule that all the enemies of Joseph Smith should be killed, and I know of many a man who was quietly put out of the way by the orders of Joseph and his Apostles while the Church was there.
>
> It has always been a well understood doctrine of

the church that it was right and praiseworthy to kill every person who spoke evil of the Prophet.

John D. Lee, *Mormonism Unveiled*, 1891.

Assassination Theology

Brigham Young brought the same assassination theology to Utah that Joseph Smith had refined in Illinois. John D. Lee relates:

> When the Danites — or Destroying Angels — were placed on a man's track, that man died — certain, unless some providential act saved him…. And I say as a fact that there was no escape for anyone that the leaders of the Church in southern Utah selected as a victim.

The Chief Justice of the Utah Supreme Court in the days of Brigham Young's rulership reports in his memoirs: "That the Danites were bound by their covenants to execute the criminal orders of the high priesthood against apostates and alleged enemies of the church is beyond question." R.N. Baskin, *Reminiscences of Early Utah*, 1914. In a court hearing held in 1889, Martin Wardell, superintendent of carpentry work for the Church for six years, was asked: "Was there anything in the oath or obligation which you took about apostasy from the Church?" Mr. Wardell replied: "Yes, you should have your throat cut and your bowels ripped out." Asked if he ever saw the penalty administered, Mr. Wardell testified:

> Yes, sir, in the latter part of 1862, about twenty miles this side of Green River, upon a man by the name of Green … three men comes up and they call upon

this man Green; he was in his wagon and didn't come out. He was a little afeard ... they pulled the man out of the wagon by the coat and he stood on his feet, and he hadn't stood more than about three minutes, — until a man took him by the hair of the head, and the other cut his throat; and when he laid down they opened his clothes and took a belt off from him with $5000. When we commenced to make trouble about it, John W. Young [a son of the prophet] told us if we didn't shut our mouths they would serve us out the same and leave us for the wolves to eat.

The leader of the squad that slit Green's throat, one W. H. Dame, explained to Wardell that Green "had apostatized from the Church once, and he had apostatized again and gone to hell now."

The Chief of the Council of the Twelve, Orson Hyde, lead apostle of the Church, delivered an address one Sunday morning in the Salt Lake tabernacle intimating that Christ Himself employed hit squads.

I will suppose a case: that there is a large flock of sheep on the prairie, and here are shepherds also, who watch over them with care. It is generally the case that shepherds are provided with most excellent dogs that understand their business.... Suppose the shepherd should discover a wolf approaching the flock, what would he do? Why, we should suppose that if the wolf was in proper distance, that he would kill him at once. In short, he would shoot him down — kill him on the spot. If the wolf was not within shot, we would naturally suppose he would set the dogs on him — and you are aware, I have no doubt, that these shepherd dogs have very pointed teeth and are very active. It is sometimes the case the shepherd, perhaps, has not with him the necessary arms to destroy the wolf, but in such a case, he would set the faithful dogs on it, and by that means accomplish its destruction.

Now, was Jesus Christ the good Shepherd? Yes; what the faithful shepherd is to the sheep, so is the Savior to his followers. He has gone, and left on the earth other shepherds who stand in the place of Jesus Christ to take care of the flock. If you say the priesthood or authorities of the Church are the shepherds, and the church is the flock, you can make your own application of this figure. It is not at all necessary for me to do it.

Journal of Discourses 1:71-72.

The portrait of Christ carrying a rifle and the apostles ranged about Him sharpening their pointed teeth reminds one of the "whittling" squads Joseph Smith employed in Nauvoo. When someone came to town he did not like, the "whittlers" would silently surround him, take out their bowie knives, and begin carving pieces of wood. Without saying a word, they escorted the unwelcome visitor to the edge of town, trailing chips and shavings behind them.

Temple Oaths in Action

Brigham Young, as the Prophet of God, stood in the place of Christ. "President Young," testified James McGuffie, who received his endowment in 1856, "was God on earth; he got the word of God and gave it to the people." As Heber C. Kimball explained: "Joseph Smith was God to the inhabitants of the earth when he was amongst us, and Brigham is God now." When the Prophet had a particularly obnoxious command to give, he would preface it with "Thus saith the Lord," acting as mouthpiece for God and eliciting blind and fanatical obedience from his oath-bound minions. "These vile tools of the Church leaders," wrote John D. Lee, who had been one himself, "were keeping their oaths of obedience to the Priesthood, and were as willing to shed blood at the command of the Prophet or any of his apostles, as ever Inquisitor was to apply the rack to an offending heretic in the dungeons of the Inquisition." (p.274) Bill Hickman, the leader of one of the assassination teams, relates that "my boys ... were of that kind that would kill father or son at the bidding of Brigham Young. This may seem strange, but there are plenty such in this country, that believe they would be doing God's service to obey, if Brigham told them to kill their own son, or the son to kill the father." *Brigham's Destroying Angel*, 1872.

In April of 1854, Jesse T. Hartley, a Salt Lake attorney, was proposed for missionary work in a church conference. Brigham Young, however, had other ideas about him. "This man Hartley," he announced, "is guilty of apostasy. He has been writing to his friends in Oregon against the church, and has attempted to publish us to the world, and should be sent to hell across lots." Hartley, apparently, had discovered a few things about the Mormons that disturbed him and had decided to get the word out. At least this is what Brigham Young believed. A month later Orson Hyde, William Hickman and a company of men were camped at a place called Fort Supply when Hartley came through. "Orson Hyde, being the head of The Twelve," Hickman writes in his memoirs, "obedience was required to his commands in the absence of Brigham Young...."

> I saw Orson Hyde looking very sour at him, and
> after he had been in camp an hour or two, Hyde told
> me that he had orders from Brigham Young, if he
> came to Fort Supply to have him used up. "Now,"
> said he, "I want you and George Boyd to do it."

Hickman and Hartley took a ride out of the camp to look for a team of horses. "Now is your time," Hyde whispered to Hickman as they left. "Don't let him come back." While crossing a deep stream, Hickman shot Hartley and his body disappeared in the water. Hickman returned to camp. "Orson Hyde told me that was well done: that he and some of the others had gone on the side of the mountain, and seen the whole performance." Mrs. Marietta V. Smith in her book, *Fifteen Years among the Mormons*, reports: "Not many days after Wiley Norton told us, with a feeling of exultation, that they had made sure of another enemy of the Church. That the bones of Jesse Hartley were in the Canons...." Judge Baskin, speaking with Hartley's brother-in-law, asked if it was true that the Mormons killed Hartley. "It was generally known," said the brother-in-law, "that Hickman had committed the crime." Asked why he did not institute proceedings, the man answered, "Don't press me for an answer to that question."

Orrin Porter Rockwell, another hit squad leader, received this cautious, yet adulatory profile, in *The Improvement Era* of 1941, the official Church magazine.

> The Mormon people of Utah today are reluctant to
> form any definite conclusions about Rockwell. He
> had such admirable qualities that his neighboring
> ranchers, Mormon or gentile, regarded him highly.
> Yet in stark contrast to this was his willingness to
> kill outlaws and criminals when he thought they

deserved it. He seemed to have no feeling for an outlaw; upon provocation he would shoot one. This method of dealing with outlaws, though an unwritten law of the early West, was so relentlessly enforced by Rockwell that it causes some of his co-religionists to frown upon him today.

Joseph Smith, for whom Rockwell originally worked, felt no such qualms. "He is an innocent and a noble boy," wrote Smith. "He was an innocent and a noble child and my soul loves him…. Let the blessings of salvation and honor be his portion." *History of the Church* V:6.

The most egregious case of Mormon murder was the Mountain Meadows massacre of 1857. The slaughter of a wagon team of 120 pioneers concluded with the holy circle that is customary when a group of Mormons administer a blessing .

> They closed in the circle, so that each man placed his left hand on the shoulder of the man nearest him and raised his right hand to the square. Each of them promised before god, angels, and their companions in this circle, that they would never under any conditions speak of this action to anyone else or to each other, and that if any did so, he would suffer his life to be taken.

A U.S. Army officer, surveying the scene of this massacre, erected a cross upon which he carved the words: "Vengeance is mine," saith the Lord, "and I will repay." When Brigham Young visited the site and saw the cross, he studied the inscription and then, raising his right arm to the square, said: "Vengeance is mine, saith the Lord, and I have taken a little of it."

Killing Apostates

As word of the fate of covenant-breakers and apostates began to spread in Salt Lake City, excitement arose, many Mormons feeling that, despite the Temple oaths, things were going too far. Brigham Young and his counselors, Heber C. Kimball and Jedediah M. Grant, sternly opposed such weak, unreligious sentiments. We have advanced beyond the point, Grant stated, where it is sufficient merely to pray to God to kill the enemies of the Church. "I want to know," he asked a Sunday congregation on March 12, 1854, "if you wish the Lord to come down and do all your dirty work?" What weaklings you are, he said. "When a man prays for a thing," he continued, "he ought to be willing to perform it himself.... Putting to death the covenant-breakers would exhibit the law of God, no matter by whom it was done — that is my opinion." Proclaimed Heber C. Kimball: "When it is necessary that blood should be shed, we should be as ready to do that as to eat an apple." *Journal of Discourses* 6:35. "To die," declared George Q. Cannon, one of the three most powerful Mormon leaders of the last decades of the nineteenth century, "is an easy thing: it is a light matter compared with apostasy." Declared Jedediah M. Grant, whose son became prophet of the Church in the 1920's and 1930's: "I not only wish but pray in the name of Israel's God, that the time was come in which to unsheath the sword, like Moroni of old, and to cleanse the inside of the platter." "I say," declared Brigham Young on March 27, 1853, "rather than that apostates should flourish here, I will unsheath my bowie knife and conquer or die."

Murder as Love: "Blood Atonement"

To allay the "whining," as Grant called it, of "the very meek, just and pious ones," the First Presidency of the Church, the supreme triumvirate of Mormonism, began to argue that enforcing the penalty on oath breakers was actually an act of mercy, not vengeance. A man who fell away from the Church after making covenants of faithfulness before God, was bound for hell. The blood of Jesus no longer cleansed him from sin. His soul could still be saved, however, declared Brigham Young, introducing a latter-day innovation in the age-old doctrine of human sacrifice, if he submitted to a ritual death at the hands of the Church. The Church had finally come full circle: murder was now an act of love. Brother Brigham pleaded with the assembled congregation:

> Will you love your brothers or sisters when they have committed a sin that cannot be atoned for without the shedding of their blood? Will you love that man or woman well enough to shed their blood? ... that is loving our neighbors as ourselves; if he needs help, help him; if he needs salvation, and it is necessary to spill his blood on the earth in order that he may be saved, spill it. That is the way to love mankind.

Journal of Discourses 4:219-220 (September 21, 1856).

Asking for a show of hands, Jedediah M. Grant stated: "I would ask how many covenant breakers there are in this city. I believe that there are a great many; and if they are covenant breakers we need a place designated where we can shed their blood." *Journal of Discourses* 4:49-50 (October 1, 1856). These killings that disturb you, explained God's Prophet, Brigham Young, are actually the actions of men animated by the spirit of God and filled with his love and mercy.

> We would not kill a man, of course, unless we killed him to save him. Do you think it would be

any sin to kill me if I were to break my covenants? Would you kill me if I break the covenants of God, and you had the spirit of God? Yes; and the more spirit of God I had, the more I should strive to save your souls by spilling your blood when you had committed sins that could not be remitted by baptism.

The Church has never abandoned this doctrine. In a pamphlet on "Blood Atonement" written in 1884, Elder Charles W. Penrose, later a member of the First Presidency, reiterated that "there are sins which men commit for which they cannot receive any benefit through the shedding of Christ's blood. Is that a true doctrine? It is true, if the bible is true. That is bible doctrine." Can such persons still be saved if the Church kills them? Are Brigham Young's sermons on blood atonement still applicable? "Do we need the same language now?" asked Elder Penrose. "I hope not; but if there was any need of it, it would be just as applicable now as then."

More than History?

The best evidence for the continuation of the practice of "sealing" members into the Church with blood covenants and then killing them for violating these covenants is the existence of the Temples themselves in the world of the 1980's. Had I not been terrorized in the Endowment Room, I would not have been impelled to investigate this bloody history. Had the Church repented of its bloody origins, it would no longer administer oaths of blood on the borders of the Washington beltway. If the Church had repudiated its murderous history, it would not be undertaking an unprecedented temple-building program around the world, aiming at having forty-one temples in full-time operation by the mid-1980's.

The Church that Joseph Smith established and that Brigham

great familiarity with Solomon Spaulding's handwriting, saw a reproduction of the portion of the original Book of Mormon manuscript attributed to "the unidentified scribe" in a Mormon publication. "What is Spaulding's handwriting doing here?" he exclaimed.

The many challenges — doctrinal, historical and literary — to Joseph Smith's claims for the Book of Mormon wearied him as a cloud of gnats does an elephant. At the dedication of the Nauvoo, Illinois temple, he produced a copy of the original manuscript to place in the cornerstone. "I've had more than enough trouble with this thing," one astonished onlooker heard him say.

More What?

When one scholar pointed out that the word "Mormon" was the same as the Greek word for "monster" ("mormo"), the prophet haughtily announced that "Mormon" was a hybrid word, part English and part Egyptian. The Egyptian word for "good" was "mon", he explained. Therefore, "Mormon" actually meant "more good."

The Prophet Translates More Ancient Writings

An English minister visited Nauvoo displaying an antique-looking manuscript containing non-English characters. He asked Joseph Smith if he could decipher them. The prophet informed him that the document was "a dictionary of Egyptian hieroglyphics, identical to those he had translated from the golden plates." The manuscript was actually a Greek version of the Psalms of David — presented on aged and moldy parchment to test the Prophet.

The Kinderhook Plates. Along the same lines, a group of Illinois citizens etched some plates with acid to represent ancient writing and buried them with some bones in the vicinity of

Kinderhook, Illinois. They then announced their find and called for the Prophet to translate. In his journal Smith's scribe at the time recorded that "President J. has translated a portion of them, and finds they contain the history of the person with whom they were found. He was a descendant of Ham, through the loins of Pharaoh, king of Egypt, and he received his kingdom from the ruler of heaven and earth."

One of the original Kinderhook plates has survived to the present time. Metallurgical tests have established that it was a hoax. The results appear in the Mormon Church magazine, the *Ensign*, of August,1981.

The Book of Abraham. In 1841, Joseph Smith began to publish his translation of the *Book of Abraham*, an Egyptian scroll found in one of two coffins containing Egyptian mummies purchased and placed on display by the Mormons as a tourist attraction. This scroll is also extant. By the early twentieth century, trained Egyptologists had declared that Smith's "translation" bore no resemblance to the funerary inscriptions on the scroll. The Church leadership in Salt Lake City, desirous of dispelling skepticism about Smith's translation recently asked a reputable Mormon Egyptologist to examine the original. He declared the translation a fake and was excommunicated. The current Church position is that the text of the *Book of Abraham*, part of the canon of scripture, was given by "inspiration" and therefore need not conform to the document from which it was "translated".

Life on other Planets

When not laboring over ancient texts, Smith on occasion disclosed truths by inspiration that were beyond the capacity of ordinary mortals to uncover. A diary of one of his associates, Oliver N. Huntington, contains a record of the following utterance by the Prophet: "The inhabitants of the moon are more of a uniform size than the inhabitants of the earth, being about six feet in height. They dress very much like the Quaker style...." Many years later Brigham Young, remembering Joseph's words, asked a Sabbath assembly: "Who can tell us of the inhabitants of this little planet that shines of an evening, called the moon?" *Journal of Discourses* 13:271.

Smith could see into heaven as well and observe the clothing worn there. "A man came to me in Kirtland," reads his journal, "and told me he had seen an angel, and described his dress. I told him he had seen no angel, and that there was no such dress in heaven." *History of the Church* V:14. Smith's vision extended not only to the moon and the heavens but to the planets as well. Christ, he told a follower, had not only come to earth but had visited Mars, Venus and all the other planets — from Mercury to Pluto. "He gave us to understand,' wrote Benjamin F. Johnson, "that there were twelve kingdoms or planets, revolving around our solar system, to which the Lord gave an equal division of His time or ministry: that now was His time to again visit the earth."

Retranslating the Bible

One of the thirteen articles of faith of Mormonism that Mormon children memorize in Sunday school is the Mormon belief that the Bible is the word of God "if translated properly" and that the Book of Mormon is also the word of God. The Mormon leadership, therefore, is free to rewrite or "retranslate" the Bible as they see fit. For example, Joseph Smith "retranslated" Jesus' saying in the Sermon on the Mount: "Judge not lest ye be judged" as "Judge not unrighteously, but judge righteous judgment."

One morning in Sunday school, a studious member raised the question as to why the Book of Mormon, translated by Joseph Smith directly from the original golden plates inscribed by ancient

American prophets, quoted Jesus as saying "Judge not lest ye be judged"? Wasn't the Book of Mormon a perfect translation "by the gift and power of God" and, therefore, unlike the Bible translations, beyond reproach? If so, why did not the words Joseph Smith corrected in the Bible not appear the same in the Book of Mormon? The teacher had no answer.

"That a quarter million of the human race," wrote J.H. Beadle in 1870, "should be led to stake their hopes for eternity on the divine authenticity of such a work, is one of the most melancholy evidences of the inherent weakness of the human intellect." *Life in Utah*, p. 255.

PART FIVE

Becoming a God

And thus I clothe my naked villainy
with old odd ends stol'n forth of holy writ,
and seem a saint, when most I play the devil.
William Shakespeare
Richard III

Ye shall be as gods.
The Serpent to Eve
Genesis 3:5

Theology of Polygamy

No leader of a vigorous movement has ever lacked for willing females desirous of trading their feminine pleasures for intimacy with a heroic celebrity. Nor did Joseph Smith. Few religious leaders, however, have created a theology to justify this activity and then enjoined it upon their followers as a practice essential to heavenly exaltation. The highest heaven in the Mormon spiritual cosmogony is the celestial kingdom, which itself contains three levels. The highest of these — the celestial of celestials — is for polygamists only. These particular individuals receive the privilege of having an eternal sex life with innumerable brides — populating worlds as yet unborn with progeny as countless as the sands of the sea.

As Brigham Young said: "Polygamy is the only religion popular in heaven, for this is the religion of Abraham, and, unless we do the works of Abraham, we are not Abraham's seed and heirs according to the promise." *Journal of Discourses* 9:322.

To followers somewhat alarmed at this new doctrine Joseph solemnly explained that an angel with a drawn sword had appeared to him and commanded him to enter the Patriarchal Order or be destroyed. A local poet phrased the situation this way:

> I once thought I had knowledge great,
> But now I find 'tis small-
>
> I once thought I'd religion, too,
> But I find I've none at all,
>
> For I have got but one lone wife,
> And can obtain no more:
>
> And the doctrine is, I can't be saved,
> Unless I've half a score.

Anon: February 7,1844.

Those with the courage and fortitude to enter into this "ancient order" would be rewarded after death by becoming, not angels, but gods. "Then shall they be gods," reads the revelation on plural marriage of July 12, 1843, "because they have no end; therefore shall they be from everlasting to everlasting because they continue. Then shall they be above all, because all things are subject unto them. Then shall they be gods, because they have all power and the angels are subject unto them."

Those who shrank from this challenge, but still remained in the Mormon church, would exist singly in their saved condition to all eternity as holy eunuchs, "ministering servants, to minister for those who are worthy of a far more and an exceeding and an eternal weight of glory: for these angels did not abide my law; therefore they cannot be enlarged, but remain separately and singly, without exaltation, in their saved condition, to all eternity, and from henceforth are not gods, but are angels of God for ever and ever."

Real-time Polygamy: Bedding Down

In April, 1843, the Prophet took his friend, Benjamin F. Johnson, for a walk and revealed to him Christ's new message. Pursuant to divine command Joseph asked that Johnson's sisters enter into the covenant. "The Lord had commanded him to take another wife," recorded Johnson in a memoir. "Among his first thoughts was to come to my mother for some of her daughters." The Prophet then explained that the parable of Jesus about the man who had one talent and hid it in the earth referred to the man who had but one wife and would not take another. He would have her taken from him and given to one who had more. Johnson letter: Journal of Wilford Woodruff, October 14, 1882.

A month later Joseph visited again and expanded on the theology of polygamy:

> Except a man and his wife enter into an everlasting covenant and be married for eternity, by the power of the Holy Priesthood, they will cease to

increase when they die, that is, they will not have any children after the resurrection.

"Before retiring," records Joseph, "I gave Brother and Sister Johnson some instructions on the priesthood," concluding with words the Church today considers holy scripture:

> In the celestial glory there are three heavens or degrees: and in order to obtain the highest, a man must enter into this order of the priesthood, and if he does not, he cannot obtain it. He may enter into the other, but that is the end of his kingdom: he cannot have an increase.
>
> *Doctrine and Covenants,* 131:1-4.

Having discoursed, he went to bed. "The prophet again came," recorded Johnson of this occasion, "and at my home occupied the same room and bed, with my sister, that the month previous he had occupied with the daughter of the late Bishop Partridge as his wife."

Joseph Jackson, conversing with Joseph's older brother, Hyrum, one evening, asked the Patriarch about one of his "spiritual" wives. "Yes," said Hyrum, "I have slept between her and my wife." "My God," said Jackson, "how did you keep them from quarreling?" "Oh," said Hyrum, "they are sisters: and that is not all, they are one in Christ Jesus."

Martha Brotherton, a young convert, perked up with delight when the Prophet invited her to a private audience. When she arrived, she found Joseph in the company of Brigham Young. The Prophet began to expound on the doctrine of eternal marriage, concluding with the opportunity for Martha to become a plural wife of Brigham Young. Martha was shocked. "What," she thought to herself, "are these men, that I thought almost perfection itself, deceivers? And is all my fancied happiness but a dream?" Joseph, seeing Martha's hesitation, sweetened the proposition. "Well, Martha," he said, "just go ahead and do as Brigham wants you to ... and if he turns you off, I will take you on." Even with this gallant offer, the young lady still declined. Joseph, displeased, did not lose his composure. He did, however, ask her to keep quiet about the whole business. "Upon your honor," said the Prophet, "you will not tell." "No sir, I will lose my life first," said Martha. "Well, that will do," said Joseph, "that is the principle we go upon." Affidavit of Martha H. Brotherton, July 13,1842 before Du Bouffay Fremon, J.P., St. Louis.

The Savior and Polygamy

To say that Jesus had made polygamy a requirement for exaltation and the privilege of becoming a god raised the question of whether the Saviour practiced the doctrine Himself. O, yes, indeed, explained Apostle Orson Hyde, that's why he was crucified.

> If Jesus Christ were now to pass through the most pious countries in Christendom with a train of women such as used to follow him, fondling about him, combing his hair, anointing him with precious ointment, washing his feet with tears, and wiping them with the hair of their heads and unmarried, or even married, he would be mobbed, tarred and feathered, and rode not on an ass, but on a rail.

Journal of Discourses 4:259. Brigham Young's Counsellor, Jedediah M. Grant, a member of the three-man First Presidency of the Church, which included the Prophet, stated the matter directly:

The grand reason of the burst of public sentiment in anathemas upon Christ and his disciples, causing his crucifixion, was evidently based upon polygamy.... A belief in the doctrine of a plurality of wives caused the persecution of Jesus and his followers.

Journal of Discourses 1:346.

Counsellor Grant cited the Second Epistle of John as evidence that the Beloved Disciple had more than one family. "The elder unto the elect lady and her children," begins the epistle, supposedly referring to one family. "The children of thy elect sister greet thee," closes the epistle, purportedly referring to a second family of the Apostle. The Saviour, as a good Mormon — indeed, a courageous and martyred preacher of the fullness of the gospel, — (It was He that administered the oaths and grips to Peter, James and John in fulfillment of which they kicked Judas to death and slew Ananias and Sapphira) this same Jesus did not leave his own wives childless, nor did his own disciples fail to heed the patriarchal call. "There are those in this audience," declared the second-in-command of the Church, George Q. Cannon, on July 2,1899 "who are descendants of the old twelve apostles — and shall I say it, yes, descendants of the Saviour Himself. His seed is represented in this body of men." The Prophet, Lorenzo Snow, in attendance, nodded his assent.

Under pressure from federal laws and Supreme Court decisions outlawing polygamy, the Mormon hierarchy compromised in 1890 and abandoned the institution in exchange for the granting of statehood to Utah. The outcry among the faithful was fierce, for they felt that political cowardice had triumphed over religious duty — and that those who abandoned polygamy for the sake of preserving the

Church would win eternal damnation for their decision — and eternal celibacy as well. In the previous decades church leaders had emphasized over and over that there was no alternative to plural marriage for a man who wanted full salvation. Apostle and later Prophet Joseph F. Smith stated on July 7, 1878:

> Some of the saints have said, and believe, that a man with one wife, sealed to him by the authority of the priesthood for time and eternity, will receive an exaltation as great and glorious, if he is faithful, as he possibly could with more than one. I want here to enter my solemn protest against this idea, for I know it is false.

In 1929, Lorin C. Woolley published an account of a visit of the Saviour to President and Prophet John Taylor in 1886. After the visit, says Woolley, reportedly an eyewitness:

> President Taylor placed his finger on the document (the manifesto forbidding plural marriage), his person rising from the floor about a foot or eighteen inches, and with countenance animated by the spirit of the Lord, and raising his right hand to the square, he said:

"Sign that document — never!"
"I would suffer my right hand to be severed from my body first."
"Sanction it — never!"
"I would suffer my tongue to be torn from its roots in my mouth before I would sanction it!"
Lorin C. Woolley, sworn statement of the events of September 27, 1886.

A fundamentalist group of Mormons, who never accepted the manifesto of 1890, claim that Jesus himself forsook the Church after this action and that is why direct revelation — so copious in the nineteenth century — has virtually ceased in the twentieth. The marriage of one man to one woman in the Temple is today considered a celestial marriage, but in terms of the original doctrine, it might better be called a lesser celestial marriage. According to Joseph Smith, no one can become a god and populate new worlds and create them as well unless he has more than one wife. Such is the law of Abraham upon which the choicest blessings of heaven are predicated. Indeed, according to the doctrine of Brother Joseph, all the Mormon wives of today will in the next world be taken from their husbands and given to polygamists. Polygamy, in fact, is something many Mormons cherish, though it is rarely discussed. "There will be polygamy after the first resurrection," one elder informed me.

Such *sub rosa* celestiality is a far cry from the thundering avowals of the founders of the church. "Now if any of you will deny the plurality of wives and continue to do so," warned Brigham Young, "I promise that you will be damned."

> The only men who become Gods, even the Sons of God, are those who enter into polygamy. Others attain unto a glory and may even be permitted to come into the presence of the Father and the Son: but they cannot reign as kings in glory, because they had blessings offered to them and they refused to accept them.

Those with the courage and wisdom to enter polygamy at times vented their disgust towards those who had only one wife. "I have noticed," said Heber C. Kimball, "that a man who has but one wife and is inclined to the doctrine, soon begins to wither and dry up, while a man who goes into plurality looks fresh, young and sprightly." Let us be real men, exhorted the Apostle. "For a man of God to be confined to one woman is small business." Apostle George A. Smith, a good friend of Joseph Smith, felt similarly. "They are a poor, narrow-minded, pinch-backed race of men," he discoursed, "who chain themselves down to the law of monogamy, and live all their days under the dominion of one wife. They ought to be ashamed of such conduct." *Journal of Discourses*, 3:291.

Adam as God

Brigham Young startled some of the faithful one day by declaring that Adam, in reality the archangel Michael, is the god of this earth "and the only god with whom we have to do." The Adam-God doctrine is a logical extension of Joseph Smith's theology of polygamy. A new world is created and populated by a god from the celestial kingdom who "comes down" with one of his wives. The movie shown in the Temple endowment ceremony, which is stopped periodically for the administration of oaths and grips, begins with a meeting between Elohim, the supreme god, and Jehovah, who is Jesus, and Michael (Adam). Professor Wolfe records an account of this portion of the sacred drama:

ELOHIM: Jehovah and Michael, there is matter unorganized. Let us go down and make a world like unto the other worlds we have created.
JEHOVAH AND MICHAEL: We will go down.

Jesus assists Michael (soon to become Adam) in "organizing the matter" and forming the earth out of chaos. But it is actually Michael's planet: Jesus is just his helper — somewhat like an elder brother helping a younger brother get started in business. With everything set — the grass, trees, animals, lakes, streams, oceans, etc. — Adam summons Eve, one of his wives (not from his rib, but from the celestial mansion) and they "go down" to the new planet and start procreating — as is their privilege since they had wisely begun their journey to eternal reproductive glory by exchanging polygamous vows on some other planet as offspring of the procreator of that planet. Having passed successfully and polygamously through that mortal probation, they now enjoyed the immortal fulfillment of becoming the heavenly father and heavenly mother of new planets of their own — originally earthly children of a celestial god and now celestial gods themselves.

When Brigham Young said that Adam is the god of this earth and "the only god with whom we have to do," he was declaring his expectation that someday he would be the god of an earth of his own and the only god with whom the people of that world would have to do. And likewise for all other faithful Mormon polygamists. As a Mormon male is god to his wife and children in this world, he will be god to entire worlds the next time around and his wives will be the various goddesses of his planetary kingdoms. "I shall have wives and children by the million," said the visionary prophet, "and kingdom after kingdom." *Journal of Discourses* 8:178. Eve, in short, was a plural wife of Adam, and all the plural wives of Mormon priests can someday be Eves too.

Christ is Born — of Adam?

To establish the godhood of the original parents — the divine procreators — Mormon theology, before application of the twentieth-century airbrush, introduced the Saviour as an essential but subsidiary personage. The planet has fallen, and elder brother Jehovah (Jesus) returns to set things straight that the children of Adam may themselves attain polygamous glory. He does so by being born of a virgin who has not known a man; she has, however, known a god. In keeping with patriarchal prerogatives this god is not the Holy Ghost but is Adam himself.

Mormons do not believe in the Immaculate Conception, nor do they believe that Jesus had a human father. Believing that "sexuality is actually an attribute of God," and that Adam is the sexual god of planet earth, they contend that Mary conceived Jesus after sexual intercourse with Adam. "Mary, the wife of Joseph," said Brigham Young, alluding to the conception of Christ, "had another husband." In the Autumn, 1967 issue of *Dialogue: A Journal of Mormon Thought*, upon whose Board of Editors sat Chase Peterson, soon to be Dean of Admissions at Harvard University, appeared an article on sex and salvation by Carlfred B. Broderick. "The eternal preservation of reproductive sexuality," began Mr. Broderick, "is the central distinguishing characteristic differentiating the exalted from the merely saved." He then explained that "the Saviour was fathered by a personage of flesh and bone."

> In light of their understanding that God is a procreating personage of flesh and bone, latter-day prophets have made it clear that despite what it says in Matthew 1:20, the Holy Ghost was not the father of Jesus.
>
> The role of the Holy Ghost was to make it possible for the mortal, Mary, to withstand the immediate presence of God.

Since a woman cannot become a goddess save as a plural wife to a god, the question arose among Mormon theologians as to whose wife Mary became. Apostle Orson Pratt speculated: "Inasmuch as God was the first husband to her, it may be that he only gave her to be the wife of Joseph while in the mortal state, and that he intended after the resurrection to take her as his wife in eternity." To Catholics, Mary is the Mother of God; to Mormons, she is one of his many wives.

Whereas some Christians may dispute the idea of the trinity, Mormons find this concept too limiting. In the theology of Mormonism, every man can be a priest and "hold all the priesthood there is," and every man can become a god as well. "We believe that the Father is god," said a Mormon doctor in 1843, "the Son is god, and the Holy Ghost is god: that makes three at least who are god, and no doubt there are a great many more." Henry Caswall, *The City of the Mormons* (1843).

Celestial Incest

Somewhat like the royal families of Europe, the Mormon potentates developed a high regard for the worth of their own blood. "Shouldn't I prefer my own blood to any other?" asserted Elder Victor Cram. "Don't I love my own blood best?" Secure in the knowledge that they were destined to be gods, the patriarchs grew reluctant to dilute the celestial blood of their descendants with the seed of the unexalted. "To have a pure priesthood," related one elder, "we may in time have to follow the example of the doves in their nest, as Christ meant it to be understood." Thus, polygamists sought out the sons and daughters of other polygamists as mates for their own children. "You will find here polygamists of the third generation," stated Elder T.H. Stenhouse. "When these boys and girls grow up, and marry, you will have in these valleys the true feeling of patriarchal life."

Articulating this distinction further, apostles sought to marry their children to the offspring of other apostles. And the prophet? Recorded one listener: "Brigham Young said he hoped the day was not far distant when ... children would be brought up to regard each other as future partners, for that thus the family would become more compact." In an interview with Brigham Young, author William Hepworth Dixon asked if the church endorsed the practice of a man marrying a widow who had a young daughter, having children by his new wife, and then marrying the daughter as well when she came of age. "This is part of the question of incest," answered the Prophet. We have no sure light on it yet. I cannot tell you what the church holds to be the actual truth: I can tell you my own opinion." Mr. Dixon then asked if Brigham Young saw any objection to the marriage of brother and sister. "Speaking for himself, not for the Church, he said he saw none at all." J.H. Beadle, *Life in Utah*: or the *Mysteries and Crimes of Mormonism* (Philadelphia, 1871); *The Mormons: the Dream and the Reality* (1857).

PART SIX

Granite Mountain

*The goal of the Genealogical Society is
to keep the temples supplied with names,*
Elder Theodore M. Burton
Assistant to the Council of the Twelve
and President of the Genealogical Society
Ensign
March, 1975

The March, 1982 issue of the *Ensign*, the glossy Church magazine, announced plans to construct ten new temples, including one in Dallas and one in Chicago, that will each have "an annual capacity for 195,000 endowments." Currently the Washington Temple is the only one east of the Mississippi, though there is one under construction in Atlanta. Los Angeles and Oakland have both had temples for a number of years. Overseas temples include one in London and one in Switzerland among others. The largest concentration of temples by far is in Utah. In 1981, over four million endowments were performed for the dead — about 200,000 per temple for each of the twenty temples currently in operation. By 1984, the Church plans to have forty-one temples constructed and in operation around the world including one recently announced for Denver, Colorado. [As of the summer of 2002, there were over 100 temples in operation, and another 20-25 planned or under construction].

Of the four million endowments done in 1981 (almost identical to the number done in 1980), only 49,800 or 1.25% were for the living. I was one of those. All the rest were for the dead. Matthew Ramage, whose name was pinned to my white jumpsuit in the Temple, was one of those.

How many of the endowments for the dead were for non-Mormons whose descendants had no knowledge of what was being done? Each Temple jurisdiction covers about four hundred wards, making each ward responsible for an average of ten endowments per week. In practice, each ward makes a Temple trip once a month on a predesignated day. Out of an active ward membership of four hundred, in my own experience about ten will regularly participate in these trips. All of these have long since been ceremonially disemboweled for all their discoverable ancestors. They suffer through the rigors of the journey and the tedium of the exercise solely to "do work for the dead," gain brownie points in heaven, and help the Bishop fill the quota. If each of the ten goes through four times in a visit, the ward can cover its forty per month quota. One elder complained to me: "I don't like going to the Temple because we rush through quickly so we can go down and get another name; I don't even get to relax a few minutes in the Celestial Room."

Based on this experience, I would estimate that of the four million endowments done annually (expected to rise to eight million with forty Temples in operation) at least 3,000,000 are of individuals who have no Mormon descendants. Where do their names come from? How did the name of Matthew Ramage, completely unknown to me, end up pinned to my jumpsuit?

The Microfilm Project

The original purpose of the Genealogical Society of the Church of Jesus Christ of Latter-day Saints was to gather together genealogical records that would assist church members in finding their ancestors and to maintain a continuously updated alphabetical index of all names endowed in the temples. The development of microfilm technology in the 1930's greatly facilitated the gathering of records. An experienced camera operator could film ten pages of parish or public records in the time that a manual transcriber would take to copy out a few lines of information — and with no problem of accuracy. By portraying themselves as careful researchers of family lineage, anxious to preserve irreplaceable records, Mormon microfilmers gained consent worldwide to film vital statistics records. By offering to provide a copy of all filmed records free of charge to co-operating institutions, many doors opened to them.

Archibald F. Bennett, secretary of the Genealogical Society of Utah in the 1930's and 1940's, and the founder of the global microfilming program, visited Connecticut in 1946 to lobby for microfilming privileges at the State Library. "Thousands of our people, including three Presidents of our church, have ancestors born in Connecticut," he said. "I myself have fifteen or twenty. We shudder to think what would happen to these records if an atom bomb were dropped on the State Library." *Ensign*, April, 1982. The state officials acquiesced and gave Bennett permission to copy the complete birth, death and marriage records of the state of Connecticut. Similar success occurred in other states and in foreign countries as well.

Granite Mountain

To store and preserve the microfilmed records, President and Prophet David O. McKay in the late 1950's ordered the construction of the Granite Mountain Records Vault, a mammoth underground nuclear bomb-proof storage facility. With seven hundred feet of solid granite overhead and steel doors weighing a total of thirty-two tons beveled inward so that even an atomic blast would only seal them tighter, the hundreds of thousands of rolls of microfilm found a secure home. (By 1982 Granite Mountain contained over a million hundred-foot rolls of microfilm containing at a minimum two billion names, and perhaps upwards of ten billion.) [Twenty years later there are 2.3 million rolls of microfilm in "The Vault."] "The gathering of all genealogically valuable records of mankind," writes a church specialist, "is the long-range goal of the Genealogical Society." *Ensign*, August,1974.

The Church estimates that about fifty billion people have lived on the earth since the creation. According to Church historians Arrington and Bitton:

> One of the most unusual structures built in recent years is the mammoth subterranean archival storage facility in Little Cottonwood Canyon, about twenty miles southeast of Salt Lake City. A huge vault bored through the sheer granite rock, this impregnable repository, with more than an acre and a half of storage area, is designed to last for centuries. It contains church records and the microfilm negatives of a vast accumulation of genealogical records — more than two billion pages of records.

Leonard J. Arrington and Davis Bitton, *The Mormon Experience* (New York, 1979), ch.14. "The air-conditioned micro-film vaults of

Utah," wrote an awestruck visiting British archivist, "with their computer control center look like something from another world." *Ensign*, August,1974.

Name Shortage

In the 1950's, the Church, heretofore primarily a Utah and Mountain States organization whose members traced their ancestors back to the original Mormon pioneers, began to enlarge its missionary work and, as a consequence, attracted a growing convert membership. As the Church developed into a substantial national and, indeed, a global institution, Prophet McKay — who had spearheaded this growth — sought to build temples outside of the Rocky Mountain region. Before he was chosen Prophet in 1951, the Church had eight temples, four in Utah, three in areas settled by the original pioneers — the Canadian Rockies, Arizona and Idaho — and one in Hawaii. In the space of four years, President McKay dedicated four more temples. The one in Los Angeles seemed like a local extension of temple facilities compared to the structures erected overseas in Switzerland, London and New Zealand. Shortly thereafter, to his dismay, the Prophet found that the new temples — insignia of the global mission of the Church — were severely underutilized. Many millions of names generated by the microfilming program were pouring into Salt Lake City every year, but Church members were not utilizing this information in sufficient numbers to provide the necessary flow of names to keep the temples active. Temple trips organized ward by ward were not difficult to arrange, but if the membership did not take the trouble to do extensive genealogical research family by family, there would be no names for them to endow once they had donned their robes.

For convert members with non-Mormon relatives and ancestors, genealogical research often ran into family hostility.

The shunned convert preferred to retreat into his new church associations rather than confront the closemouthed displeasure of the great aunt who knew the whole story of his family's history but adamantly refused to cooperate. At the same time this phenomenon was stifling genealogical research and therefore keeping the member away from the temples (since he had no family names to endow), the microfilm kept cascading into Church headquarters. Somewhere in this mountain of filmed records were the names and dates of the ancestors the frustrated convert could not identify. Without some family guidance, however, the member — even were he capable of searching effectively in these records — would have had no clue as to where to look.

In this project the Church refused to help. Professional genealogists were very expensive to employ; the Church lay the burden on the members. The members threw their hands up in helplessness at a task that often frustrated professionals, and temple work dwindled. As the Church later expressed it: "The Genealogical Society cannot do the research work of establishing family lines of priesthood heritage which God has assigned the Priesthood to do." *Ensign*, May, 1975. The Genealogical Society existed to gather names, the raw data, but the rest was up to the members. Elder Theodore M. Burton, President of the Genealogical Society, stated the matter baldly: "The Genealogical Society," he stated, "does not do genealogical research work." The Church wouldn't do it; the members couldn't do it — and the beautiful temples grew still.

To solve the problem of lagging genealogical research by the membership without shouldering the expense of providing professional research help to millions of Mormons, the Prophet ordered the Genealogical Society to extract names directly from the microfilmed records for use in temple endowments — without any concern as to whether the names extracted were those of ancestors

of church members. A name was a name. This ominous development, unheralded and unannounced, silently broke faith with the
hundreds of records custodians who had co-operated with the
Mormon microfilming program. Archibald Bennett's heart-stirring
plea for preservation of the records of his ancestors appeared somewhat duplicitous in light of President McKay's decision to use the
obtained records indiscriminately to keep the temples active. The
members would not do enough genealogical research to keep the
temples busy? Very well. All they had to do was go to the temples
and the Church would provide the names for them. Thus, Matthew
Ramage's name came out of the computer and was pinned on my
jumpsuit.

Controlled Extraction

Once this solution proved successful, the microfilming
program was accelerated. The Genealogical Society trained
members worldwide in microfilming techniques, dubbing them
"research specialists" and equipping them with the credential
"Accredited Genealogist (A.G.)" to disarm records custodians. The
extracting of names from the growing microfilm files was
controlled as follows:

> A corps of young women was gathered and
> trained to read Old English parish registers
> projected from a 16-mm film onto a screen in a
> film reader. The data from these registers was flex-
> otype code-punched to paper tape and simultane-
> ously transmitted to a computer two blocks away,
> under a dual "match-merge" system of reading and
> code punching of entries by two persons. With this
> system, any errors were immediately detected and
> could be corrected, which practically eliminated

the chance for errors.

With the R-Tab (records tabulation) system, millions of identified names are continually fed into the computer mass file and then sent on to the temples for ordinance work. The system, together with the very extensive filming program, will insure an adequate supply of names for as many temples as may be constructed, so long as any records remain extant for filming.

Hoyt Palmer, "For Those Who are Waiting,"
Ensign, August, 1974.

The process of culling names from the microfilmed records is known as "controlled extraction," as in "the controlled extraction program being carried on in many of the stakes of the Church with such great devotion and success." *Ensign*, May, 1982. The term "controlled" means simply that by having the records "extracted" simultaneously by two clerks, errors and oversights are eliminated. The "extract" is "controlled" to make sure the records are accurately picked clean.

The Church takes seriously its mission to allow every soul in the Spirit World the option of accepting a proxy endowment. Elder Theodore M. Burton stated frankly in 1975: "The First Presidency has charged the Genealogical society to provide enough names to keep the temples in operation. The system developed in response to the request is called the controlled extraction program." *Ensign*, March,1975. "The members of the Church today," wrote the President of the Genealogical Society in 1975, "are producing only 34 percent of the names used in temple ordinance work. The remainder are supplied by controlled extraction." He concluded that "the general trend is towards an increase in the number of names submitted to temples through the Society."

In 1968 member or "patron" names endowed in the temples came to 600,000. Controlled extraction provided 1,100,000 more. Had the Church only patron input to utilize, each of the thirteen temples in operation in 1968 would have had only 46,000 names to process, less than 25% of capacity. By feeding in 1,100,000 non-Mormon-related names, culled from parish and public records, utilization rose to 70%. The feed from the Granite Mountain Vault rose and fell as needed to augment patron input and keep the endowment rooms busy. In 1974, for example, 2.4 million endowments were performed, two-thirds of which had no connection with member research. *Ensign*, March, 1975.

In light of this data, the statement of Apostle Gordon B. Hinckley in the August, 1974 *Ensign* that "the primary purpose (of the genealogical records preservation program) is to afford members of the Church the resources needed to identify their dead ancestors," is not correct. The primary purpose of the records acquisition program is to provide names for proxy baptisms, an objective that does not require any genealogical research whatsoever by the membership.

Notwithstanding the power of controlled extraction, patron input is still encouraged strongly. "As new temples are being constructed in ever greater rapidity," said Elder Burton in an address to the April, 1975 General Conference, "we are faced with the problem of keeping them in operation." In General Conference seven years later — April, 1982 — the same refrain was repeated by Elder W. Grant Bangerter. "It would be unfortunate," he said, "to build temples around the earth and have them stand largely idle." Members should not look upon the temples simply as a place "to do a name." Going to the temple to endow extractees, stated Wayne Brickey, supervisor of priesthood genealogy textbooks, is "vital," but "many of us seem to confine ourselves to that part — and even at that, the temples are well below capacity attendance." Don't depend on controlled extraction to do it all, exhorted Elder Brickey. Go out and find your own "Every ancestor found is a victory; every name submitted is a soul with an opportunity for exaltation." Having encouraged, the patrons, he then reverted to hard facts:

> As temples become more busy and more numerous, it will be necessary to extract an enormous number of names from various records in the world, on a careful, controlled basis, in order to supplement those names submitted privately by Church members. This work has already begun, but it will undoubtedly grow, allowing a much greater amount of temple work to be done.

Wayne Brickey, "The New Scope of What We have Called Genealogy," *Ensign*, January, 1977.

What, Already Endowed?

New church members who desire to stand in for their ancestors are often dismayed to discover that the endowment has already been done through controlled extraction. The Genealogical Society sought to put a positive spin on this situation. All you have to do, says Elder Burton, is to check our alphabetical print-out of controlled extraction endowments. If it's already been done, you can relax in the knowledge that your ancestor has already received "the saving ordinances." Elder Burton expressed puzzlement that anyone should be offended at endowment by extraction. "Why," he asks, "do some Saints feel hurt when they find we are doing work for them that saves them time and money?"

Nothing ... could be more helpful to the Saints than

to have all the tedious spadework in Church and vital records done for them at reduced cost through the controlled extraction program. It is not a handicap, but a blessing to the Saints.

Ensign, March, 1975. The members may be pardoned for their displeasure upon discovering that beloved ancestors for whom they desired to stand as proxy were endowed by an unknown individual to fill the quota one Saturday in a distant ward.

If Mormons are sometimes offended at the impersonality of the controlled extraction process, the feelings of non-Mormons about their ancestors, who are yearly endowed by the millions, might surprise Elder Burton even more.

With controlled extraction in full swing, and all the wards organized for monthly temple trips to stand proxy for the computer output, no obstacle remained to the erection of more and more temples. The ceremonial disembowelment of the entire human race is now well underway. "We thank Thee, O God, for a Prophet" begins a popular Mormon hymn, "to guide us in these latter days."

Celebrity Endowments

Before the inauguration of the controlled extraction program, the Church on an ad hoc basis performed endowments by proxy for selected non-Mormons who had passed on. The endowment work for George Washington and the other founding fathers was done for them in a Utah temple in the nineteenth century. Spencer W. Kimball, Prophet of the Church and grandson of Heber C. Kimball, declared in the January,1977 *Ensign*:

We know that the spirit world is filled with the spirits of men who are waiting for you and me to get

> busy — waiting as the signers of the Declaration of
> Independence waited. "Why," they asked President
> Wilford Woodruff, "why do you keep us waiting?"

Although the Church will not do genealogical research for its members, it makes an exception for non-members of royal lineage. The Royalty Identification Unit (Special Services Section) of the Genealogical Department maintains a custom-produced list of celebrity endowments that are not part of the controlled extraction print-out. These names are listed in the T99 (Special Handling) file — "royalty and other special records processed by the Genealogical Society." The Church reserves to itself the right to perform the ordinances for the great and discourages any member from standing as proxy for a royal forebear. "Due to the complexities of research associated with royalty," reads a Genealogical Society Research Paper (Series F, No.4), "the Genealogical Department researches these lines. Therefore, when a family's ancestors are individuals with royal titles, it is recommended that church members spend their resources on other lines that need to be researched."

To emphasize that the Church's allotment of its own resources to genealogical research is solely for the purpose of preparing blue-blood endowments, the following warning is added: "Caution: the spouses of royalty may have been common people and therefore may not be traced as part of the royalty identification projects."

Despite Elder Burton's statement to the contrary ("The Genealogical Society cannot do the research work of establishing family lines of priesthood heritage which God has assigned the priesthood to do"), the Genealogical Society does do such research, but only for nobility. God, it appears, has assigned the "common" priesthood the task of finding their own undistinguished forebears, but reserves to Himself through His Church the establishing and endowing of the crowned heads of Europe.

If this practice is part of the Restored Gospel, then, despite what the Bible says, God is a "respecter of persons" — "Special Handling" for the aristocracy; mass extractions for the rest of us. "Blessed are the poor, for theirs is the kingdom of heaven" — if they can find it. "Blessed are the rich and famous, for theirs is the kingdom of heaven" — courtesy of the Genealogical Society of the Church of Jesus Christ of Latter-day Saints. The average working saint, who faithfully pays his tithe and devotes many hours per week to church work, is periodically exhorted to "search out" his ancestors — an expensive and time-consuming undertaking. Were he an aristocrat, the Church would do it for him free of charge.

George II. Along with the Founding Fathers in the T99 file are the kings of England. George II of England, according to information in a Genealogical Society Research Paper, received a proxy baptism on September 5, 1893 during the reign of the Prophet Wilford Woodruff. His wife, Queen Caroline, was baptized the same day. Their children also enjoyed a Mormon proxy baptism — some on September 5, 1893 and the rest a week later on September 12th. On September 20, 1893, Queen Caroline received her endowment through a female proxy who pledged her to devote all her time, talent and substance to the Mormon Church, performed the secret handshakes on her behalf and took the oaths and penalties for her.

Let us say that Queen Caroline joyfully received these ordinances in the Spirit World where she had been stuck in limbo for over one hundred years since her death, and immediately left spirit prison to be with Christ. Sad to say, George II could not go with her, for his endowment was not performed until June 4, 1924 — over thirty years later. Why the Mormon authorities made him wait, I do not know. The royal couple and their children are now an eternal family: the sealing of children to parents occurred January 14, 1935.

Having lived and died ignorant of the advent of the restored gospel, King George can now enjoy the bliss of celestial glory — and, hopefully, when the opportunity arises, have other wives sealed to him in a latter-day temple, whereupon he may begin to create and populate new planets.

If George and Caroline can become Adam and Eve to new worlds, instead of being confined in spirit prison all their eternal days, surely they owe Joseph Smith and his successors a tremendous debt of gratitude. It is nice to know that Christ through his priesthood on earth takes special care of European aristocrats who were also very well taken care of while here on earth.

New England Bluebloods. We all know of Boston, "the land of the bean and the cod, where the Lowells talk only to the Cabots, and the Cabots talk only to God." Eight of the Cambridge, Massachusetts Cabots did not have the opportunity of talking with God until May 24, 1975 when they received their controlled extraction endowments in the Tempe, Arizona Temple, having been baptized there four weeks previously. The oldest was Anna Sophia Blake Cabot, born July 2, 1796; the youngest Jane Lawrence Cabot, born November 23, 1846. Three days later — April 29, 1975 — seven more Cambridge Cabots won the privilege at the Arizona Temple of entering into the presence of Christ — ranging from Frederick Cabot, born February 20, 1788, to George B. Gay Cabot, born April 8, 1836. Surely they are all everlastingly grateful to the state of Massachusetts for its willingness to participate in the Latter-day Saints microfilming program.

Should the Cambridge Lowells desire to talk to these Cabots, they need not despair, for they too have been extracted. While the Cabots were being endowed in Arizona, three Lowells — Anna Cabot Lowell (b. September 29, 1811), Augustus Lowell (b. January 15, 1830) and Blanche Lowell (b. 1847) — received their baptisms and proto-Masonic blood oaths in the Washington, D.C.

Temple.

Frank J. Cannon, former Senator from Utah and son of First Counsellor George Q. Cannon, records in his memoirs a story about Theodore Roosevelt:

> And it is told — sometimes solemnly, sometimes with a grin — that, in the Temple at Salt Lake, a proxy has stood for him and he has been baptized into the Mormon Church; that proxies have stood for the members of his family and that they have been sealed to him; and finally that proxies have stood for some of the great queens of the past (who had not already been sealed to Mormon leaders) and that they have been sealed to the President for eternity!

Roosevelt had done a great favor to the Mormon Church in helping to secure a vote in the Senate seating polygamist Reed Smoot after a Senate Investigation Committee had recommended that he be denied admission. "It is not uncommon practice in the Mormon Church," explains Frank Cannon, "thus to 'do a work' for a Gentile who has befriended the people or otherwise won the gratitude of the Church authorities." Frank J. Cannon and Harvey J. O'Higgins, *Under the Prophet in Utah* (Boston, 1911).

Controlled Deception

Should offended non-Mormons oppose continuation of the controlled extraction program and lobby for an end to Mormon microfilming privileges in public and church records, a trained Mormon theologian may well challenge them: are the millions who died without benefit of having the opportunity to accept the restored gospel to be prevented from enjoying the ultimate in heavenly bliss simply because their living descendants refuse to do the work for them, or allow others to do it in their stead? Is this fair to the dead? "There are uncounted millions," wrote Gordon B. Hinckley, then an apostle and now a counsellor to the Prophet, in the August, 1974 *Ensign*, "who have walked the earth and who have never had the opportunity to hear the gospel. Shall they be denied such blessings as are offered in the temples of the church?" A Mormon "genealogist" told me candidly:

> We say we're microfilming the records as part of a genealogical research project, but it has nothing to do with that. We just need names to do endowments. Our work won't be done until everyone that ever lived upon the earth is endowed. Whether they accept the work that we do for them here is up to them.

I can imagine the response if B'nai B'rith representatives were to go to the Connecticut State Library and make copies of vital statistics records under the guise of doing genealogical research into Jewish roots, and then used these records wholesale for secret rituals converting the ancestors of every living Connecticut resident to Judaism — with the active intention of doing this to every Gentile person that ever lived. Surely the activities of such a cult would be restrained. It is quite possible that in the millions of illicit endowments for non-Mormon deceased at least a few Jews have been ritually converted to Mormonism. [In May, 1995, the Church signed an agreement with major Jewish organizations and expunged the endowments of 360,000 holocaust victims from its records. Gary Mokotoff, "The Mormon/Jewish Controversy: What Really Happened," *Avotaynu*, Summer, 1995 (www.avotaynu.com/mormon.htm)] I doubt that any of the millions of Christians whose ancestors have been secretly converted to

Mormonism would be any less upset were they to find out what has been going on in the Temples of the Lord. [The Catholic Bishop of Salt Lake said he did not think Joan of Arc would mind. *Salt Lake Tribune*, October 9, 1999.] The only solace I have in knowing that the Russian Communists obliterated my ancestors' graves in Lemburg, Poland, is that no hungry Mormon name-robber, looking for records of dead persons to feed the ghoulish endowment factories, will ever be able to uncover any trace of them.

PART SEVEN

Kingdom Come

What the world calls "Mormonism" will rule every nation.
God has decreed it, and his own right arm will accomplish it.
Chief Apostle Orson Hyde
Journal of Discourses, VII, 48-53

Mormonism is neither a fraternal order nor a religious association: it is a kingdom, the kingdom of God. In the words of Joseph F. Smith, sixth Prophet of the Church:

> The greatest event that has ever occurred in the world, since the resurrection of the Son of God from the tomb and his ascension on high, was the coming of the Father and the Son to that boy Joseph Smith, to prepare the way for the laying of the foundation of his kingdom — not the kingdom of man — never more to cease nor to be overturned.

The kingdom "never more to cease nor to be overturned" is the messianic kingdom foreseen in the second chapter of the Book of Daniel:

> And in the days of these kings shall the God of heaven set up a kingdom, which shall never be destroyed: and the kingdom shall not be left to other people, but it shall break in pieces and consume all these kingdoms, and it shall stand forever.

Stated Church historian B.H. Roberts:

> We are warranted in the belief, however, that it will be a tangible, *bona fide* government of God on earth, consisting of a king; subordinate officers; laws; subjects; and the whole earth for its territory — for its dominion.

History of the Church, Vol. I, Intro. p. xxxvi. The Mormons equate this kingdom as well with the words of Revelation 11:15: "The kingdoms of this world are become the kingdoms of our Lord, and of His Christ: and He shall reign forever and ever."

"The kingdom is organized," wrote Brigham Young in 1844, "and although as yet no bigger than a grain of mustard seed, the little plant is in a flourishing condition and our prospects brighter than ever." *Id.,* Vol. VII, p.381-Note. Few Americans comprehended the magnitude of the political expectations of the Mormons. "As was observed by Brother Pratt, that kingdom is actually organized and the inhabitants of the earth do not know it," stated Brigham Young on July 8,1855. "If this people know anything about it, all right; it is organized preparatory to taking effect in the due time of the Lord, and in the manner that shall please him." *Id.*

Joseph Smith, capitalizing on the fervor for primitive Christianity that animated the American frontier in the 1820's and 1830's, claimed that Jesus Christ Himself had chosen him to restore His original ceremonies, build up a Church to greet Him at the Second Coming, and rule the earth during the Millennium. "Flee the wrath to come" and "gather to Zion" were the watchwords of Mormon missionaries in the early days. "The missionary was confident the end of the world was hourly approaching," wrote one observer, "that soon the earth and all therein, except such as embraced Mormonism, would be destroyed, and his benevolence made him use extraordinary exertions to bring the human race within the pale that he assured them could alone save them from impending destruction." William White Smith, *The Prophets* (1855).

Although the Mormons argue that the church of God will be distinct from the government of God during the Millennium, this is true only in the sense that the communist party of the Soviet Union was different from the government of Russia after the revolution of 1917. Brigham Young did say that the "kingdom grows out of the Church of Jesus Christ of Latter-day Saints, but it is not the church." He also said, however, that "no one can draw the line between the government of God and the government of the children of men." *History of the Church*, Vol. VII, p.382; April 9, 1844. In fact, although non-Mormons may participate in the rulership of the millennial kingdom, the Mormon priesthood will control its organization and administration. The kingdom of God and the church of God will both be run by the Mormon Church — under the direction of Christ, who will pass freely back and forth "through the veil" during this period.

"What I mean by the kingdom of God," wrote Joseph F. Smith in October, 1906, "is the organization of the Church of Jesus Christ of Latter-day Saints, over which the Son of God presides, and not man.

That is what I mean." On another occasion he said, "I know that this is the kingdom of God and that God is at the helm." It is such claims that inspired Apostle Parley Pratt to say of Joseph Smith: "His work will live to endless ages. Unnumbered millions yet unborn will mention his name with honor." Grieving at the blindness of humanity in failing to recognize the nascent kingdom in their midst, Apostle Ezra Taft Benson wrote in 1948: "The history of humanity has, to a large extent, been one of groping blindly in the dark, fearing for the future and yet resisting the guiding hand of inspired men who would willingly lead mankind in the path of safety." Forward to W. Cleon Skousen, *Prophecy and Modern Times* (1948). At the head of the path stands Joseph Smith, holder of the keys of salvation — "keys which will unlock the door into the kingdom of God to every man who is worthy to enter and which will close that door against every soul that will not obey the law of God." It can hardly be expected that Christ will allow the governance of His kingdom to rest in the hands of those who refuse to acknowledge His chosen medium of salvation. "No man or woman in this dispensation," declared Brigham Young, "will ever enter into the celestial kingdom of God without the consent of Joseph Smith." *Journal of Discourses* 7:289.

Well known and often cited within the church is the utterance of Joseph Smith that "the day will come when the Constitution of the United States hangs by a thread — and will be saved only by the elders of the Church." One student of Mormonism phrased this expectation somewhat differently: "They are promising their followers," wrote Bruce Kinney in 1912, "that they will in time control things politically in the United States." *Mormonism: the Islam of America.* Mormon political activity is rooted in the assumption that the day is coming when the American political system will collapse and the hierarchical apparatus of the Mormon Church will take its place. The Mormon Church, in this sense, is a shadow government — like the ayatollahs of Iran — only awaiting the Biblically-predicted chaos that shall sweep away American democracy and install Mormon theocracy in its place — to reign forever, "never more to be overturned." A commonly-cited scenario envisions the inevitable degeneration of the godless American polity into the anarchy envisioned by Christ in his discourse on the Mount of Olivet: "Nation shall rise up against nation and kingdom against kingdom.... Now the brother shall betray the brother to death, and the father the son; and children shall rise up against their parents and cause them to be put to death." Mark 13:8, 12.

Joseph Smith added his own personal vision to this prophecy: "I saw men hunting the lives of their own sons, and brother murdering brother, women killing their own daughters, and daughters seeking the lives of their mothers."

The principle of "gathering to Zion as God pours out His wrath" is fundamental to Mormonism. Current policy is that Mormons should stay in their own localities, not migrate to Salt Lake City, but "build up Zion" where they live. When the time comes, however, the Prophet shall summon all Mormons everywhere to gather in to Salt Lake City for shelter while the Great Anarchy sweeps the globe. After the Great Wrath, Christ Himself shall return, appearing first in a Mormon Temple in Independence, Missouri on a plot of ground designated by Joseph Smith for this purpose. This Temple shall be the centerpiece of a holy city, the New Jerusalem of Revelation 21, which shall surround it and become the new capital of Mormonism. From it the world shall be ruled as the Mormons who fled to Salt Lake City for protection return to their hometowns and home lands as rulers and organizers of the new and everlasting theocratic kingdom. Although Christ will also appear in Jerusalem to organize the repentant and worshipful Jews into the Millennial Kingdom, the real seat of world government will be the New Jerusalem in Missouri. The two capitals will be formally co-equal, but the New Jerusalem will be the source of power, much as the Disney Corporation is to Disneyland. The new Jewish kingdom will require instruction, guidance and ultimately subordination to the Mormon authorities, for he who receives authority from another is subservient to the giver of that authority. The Jews can only receive the authentic priesthood of God from the Mormons, and therefore, must be beholden and obedient to them.

Yes, the messianic kingdom described by Isaiah is already here in embryo in Utah; the Jews shall be part of it — indeed, it cannot achieve its fullness until they do — but they will not rule it. That question was decided in 1820 when Christ appeared to Joseph Smith and gave him the Keys of the Millennium. In the 1830's one dramatic day Moses and Elijah also came to visit and invested the Prophet Joseph with their authority as well. "And it shall come to pass in the last days," reads Isaiah 2:2, "that the mountain of the Lord's house shall be established in the top of the mountains, and shall be exalted above the hills; and all nations shall flow unto it." In the annotated Mormon edition of the Bible, the mountains here are the Rocky Mountains and "the Lord's house" is the Salt Lake Temple. "For out of Zion shall go forth the law" continues Isaiah, supposedly referring to the Mormon capital, "and the word of the Lord from Jerusalem," the Jewish capital.

The Mormons have quite a message for Messianic Jews — quite a message — and someday, no doubt, if they get their hands on the levers of power, they will attempt to deliver it — first as protectors of the Jews and then as their rulers.

Before the Church became a national institution and began to soften and obscure its publicly-displayed doctrines, the inevitable consolidation of all earthly power into the hands of the Mormon authorities was clearly understood. "The understanding," related

Bishop Cahoon in his testimony, "was that God had established His Kingdom upon the earth, and the Mormon Church was the Kingdom of God, and all that belonged to the Mormon Church were expected to yield allegiance to that church, to that Kingdom alone, and the highest allegiance was to the Mormon Church — the Kingdom of God." An oath administered in the endowment ceremony at that time committed the priesthood to "avenge the blood of the prophets" and teach this doctrine to their children and their children's children. The Church "taught," testified Bishop Cahoon, "that this government would be overthrown, and the Kingdom of God be established on its ruins.... They didn't care much about the government of the United States when they had a kingdom." The comparable oath that I took in the Mormon Temple in Washington, D.C., in August, 1981 had no political overtones but did commit me to pledge all my time talent and treasure to the upbuilding of the Church of Jesus Christ of Latter-day Saints. Such an oath does not leave much room for any other loyalty.

The official establishment of the government of God as distinct from the government of the Church took place in 1844 when Joseph Smith organized a secret Council of Fifty as the ruling politburo of the kingdom of God. This council encompassed non-Mormons, including Joseph Jackson, who, by his own report, was offered $3,000 by the Prophet to kill the governor of Missouri. In the days before the authority of the United States government became effective in Utah, the Council of Fifty, according to church historians Leonard J. Arrington and Davis Bitton, "began deliberations on the nature of civil government to be established in the valley." Having ruled the Salt Lake valley directly through the church, Brigham Young and his associates now decided to establish a civil government subsidiary, nominally independent of the church, called the State of Deseret. On March 8,1849, three days after the opening of the constitutional convention, a standard state constitution of the time was adopted — and an election scheduled for two months later to select officers for the new state. Ballots, however, were actually cast four days later on March 12,1849 — somewhat limiting the amount of campaigning any independent candidate might undertake. Brigham Young won the office of governor and Heber C. Kimball chief justice, both winning 100% of the ballots cast for their respective offices. The election of the temporal government of the Kingdom of God had as much resemblance to a free election as the elections conducted by the governments of Eastern Europe in 1946. This procedure was deliberate. "Every government lays the foundation of its own downfall," declared Brigham Young in 1872, "when it permits what are called democratic elections." "Remember," said the church authority who interviewed me for my worthiness to become a Mormon priest, "the Church is a theocracy, not a democracy." Any government the church creates, it creates in its own image.

All power lies with the Prophet who is God's representative on earth; his word is law. As the Prophet is to the Church, so the Bishop is to the local ward. Unlike the rabbi of a Jewish congregation, who is dependent upon the favor of the synagogue for his position, the Bishop is chosen and installed solely by his ecclesiastical superiors. The notion of "division" or "separation" of powers is anathema to Mormonism.

The members of the ward are sternly enjoined to "sustain the authorities" for this is the "only true" church of God and the officers of it God's chosen — selected by "inspiration" after "prayerful consideration," and installed by the laying on of hands. To dispute the church authorities is to defy God. And who would do that?

Thus, it is not surprising that, given the occasion and the opportunity, the Mormon hierarchy will create a civil government in the image of their church government — elections by acclamation and zealous obedience the essence of virtue. The popularity of military careers for Mormon youth is a direct outgrowth of the inculcation of these principles. That the Mormons fully expect to rule the United States and the world as well one day is, of course, a political hallucination that could never happen. If so, however, it may be expected that they will formally reverence the U.S. Constitution while simultaneously abolishing the division of powers, based on mistrust of all unchecked human authority, that underlies it. A portion of Bishop Cahoon's testimony, given in 1889, expresses the sentiments that still reign in the minds of the Mormon authorities:

Q. Did they ever teach you anything in regard to the overthrowing of the Constitution of the United States, did you ever hear that at all?

A. The Constitution of the United States would be, perhaps, an after consideration; after the government was overthrown the leaders of the Mormon Church would reform that document to suit themselves.

Q. Did you ever hear them say that the document needed reforming?

A. O, yes.

Q. You never heard it taught that that was a Divine Document?

A. O, yes, they taught that it was an inspired document, but that it would be better — eventually it would be better.

Q. Who was going to better it?

A. The priesthood of the Mormon Church.

Q. When?

A. Well, when they got it in their hands.

Q. When was that going to be?

A. Well, directly, it has been put off from time to time. They say it is pretty near now.

Q. State when and where you heard it.

A. Heard it all the while, ever since I was in the church.

To obscure the fundamental incompatibility of Mormon doctrine with democratic politics, Brigham Young made the remarkable statement: "The Constitution and laws of the United States resemble a theocracy more closely than any government now on earth." *Journal of Discourses* 6:342. He came slightly closer to the truth in the following statement:

> Few, if any, understand what a theocratic government is. In every sense of the word, it is a republican government, and differs but little in form from our National, State, and Territorial Governments; but its subjects will recognize the will and dictation of the Almighty....
>
> *Id.*

There is no room for legitimate disagreement in Mormonism. Anyone who questions church practices is considered to have lost his faith in revealed truth. Such an individual must speedily repent and humble himself, begging forgiveness or he will be excommunicated. A man named Morris had the effrontery to establish his own mini-Mormonism in Utah in the days of Brigham Young, claiming to receive instructions from God as did the Mormon prophet. Brigham sent his "avenger" on horseback and shot the fledgling prophet dead in broad daylight in the presence of his followers. John Taylor, successor to Brigham Young as Prophet, made it clear that the Mormons envision no separation of church and state once they take power.

Was the kingdom that the Prophets talked about, that should be set up in the latter times, going to be a Church? Yes. And a state? Yes, it was going to be both Church and State, to rule both temporarily *(sic)* and spiritually.

When Utah became a state and began to elect Senators and Congressmen, some question arose as to whether a Mormon Senator would consider himself bound by his oath to support the Constitution and laws of the United States, or whether his endowment oaths of supreme loyalty to the Church would prevail. John Taylor answered as follows:

It may be asked, How can we live under the dominion and laws of the United States and be subjects of another kingdom? Because the kingdom of God is higher, and its laws are so much more exalted than those of any other nation, that it is the easiest thing in life for a servant of God to keep any of their laws and, as I have said before, this we have uniformly done.

Journal of Discourses 6:24. The Mormon leadership fully expect the American government to collapse as a prelude to their assumption of power on the American continent. "When the Lord commands it through his living prophets," writes a BYU faculty member in the June, 1976 *Ensign*, "the New Jerusalem will become the capital city…." The Constitution will then become the responsibility of the Church of Jesus Christ of Latter-day Saints. "It is not wise to sit by and think that the protection of the Constitution is the problem of someone else at some other time," warns the *Ensign*. "Our commission to save the Constitution is, like salvation, a continuing task." Should the Mormon apparatus ever come to power in the United States during a period of inner turmoil, this country will become a white tyranny, the ecclesiastical mirror image of communism. "And this is the redemption of Zion," said Joseph Smith in 1841, "when the saints shall have redeemed that government and reinstated it in all its purity and glory."

The Mormons will come as saviors of the constitution, firm-willed virtuous patriots full of love for God and country. Their ecclesiastical autocracy will come wrapped in the evocative symbolism of constitutional purification.

But, of course, it could never happen here. Joseph Smith was but twenty-five years of age, full of the fire of youth, when he donned the mantle of prophethood: Brigham Young was forty-seven. There has not been a prophet under the age of sixty since. The Church is a mature businesslike institution that discourages excessive fanaticism. Its doctrines have been softened and blended to have as wide an appeal as possible. Tradition since World War II has chosen the oldest apostle for the office of Prophet. Of the five prophets since 1945, four were in their mid-seventies when chosen and the fifth over ninety. The current Prophet, Spencer W. Kimball, is eighty-seven: his two counsellors are eighty-four and eighty-five. The Church in many of its activities today displays a silly farcical spirit — a spirit I always found offensive but now view as inherent in a company of religious play actors. Gordon B. Hinckley, who was recently elevated from the Council of the Twelve Apostles to be a third counsellor to the Prophet, was active in the 1970's as an adviser to the Public Communications Department — the Church's propaganda agency. [In 1995, Hinckley became the 15th President and Prophet of the Church.] He worked, in particular, on the "subject content" for the Washington, D.C. Visitor's Center, which is attached to the Temple.

In the Washington center, life-size mannequins representing Isaiah, Nephi, Joseph Smith, and other prophets will speak their messages from the scriptures. With translucent masks and hidden rear projection, the figures will speak as living oracles.

Ensign, August, 1974.

One does not associate such Disneyland techniques with traditional religious solemnity. They remind one more of Revelation, Chapter 13: "And he had power to give life unto the image of the beast, that the image of the beast should both speak, and cause that as many as would not worship the image of the beast should be killed." Whether the Wizards of Mormon will one day install a humanoid mannequin as prophet is beyond my power to foresee. Whether or not a young ambitious technocrat prophet will be able to simulate the second coming of Christ and gather an ocean of white-robed believers to the templed Missouri hills to witness the inauguration of the Millennium is also beyond my power of prediction. A visit to the Hill Cumorah pageant staged every summer in Palmyra, New York to commemorate and re-enact Joseph Smith's discovery of the golden plates from which he translated the Book of Mormon will keep interested observers of the Millennial Kingdom up to date on the state of the art in religious pyrotechnics, while we wait patiently for the Mormon "rendezvous with our Constitution's destiny." *Ensign*, June, 1976.

Conclusion

And I John saw the holy city, new Jerusalem,
coming down from God out of heaven,
prepared as a bride adorned for her husband.

...

And I saw no temple therein.
Book of Revelation
Chapter 21

It has not been easy to tell the truth about the Church of Jesus Christ of Latter-day Saints — to conduct a controlled extraction of the teeth of this cunning dragon. The Ku Klux Klan, by comparison, is a model of sincerity. Under the pretense of "bearing a message from Jesus Christ," Mormon missionaries seek to lure the unwary into an oath-bound organization from which there is no escape except on terror of death. At least an initiate into the Ku Klux Klan understands the nature of the institution he is joining. A Mormon convert, however, as he prepares for his momentous and soul-stirring first trip to the Temple, is told that he will enter an atmosphere of "simplicity, dignity and quiet ... there to ponder quietly the eternal things of God." "There is a feeling of timelessness and peace found there that exists nowhere else," writes BYU Stake President and Professor of Physics J. Duane Dudley. "The only way to prepare for the temple," he continues, "is to prepare your spiritual self. You should go to the temple in a spiritual frame of mind and be ready to learn spiritually." There is little in such language to prepare the novice for irrevocable membership in a secret society sealed by blood oaths. The fact that so few have publicly revealed the truth about Mormonism is an indication of the effectiveness of the terror instilled in the Endowment rooms. So sinuous and seductive is the preparation for this experience that the initiate is baffled, embarrassed and terrified to admit that he has been taken in and played for a sucker. (He also may be too busy adjusting to the discomfort of wearing his Mormon underwear continuously to think about much else.) If he wavers or quavers, his priesthood leaders will hover over him. "He is having trouble with his testimony," they will say and spend time "prayerfully" re-educating the weakling and carefully exclude him from any position of responsibility in the apparatus.

An indication that other first-time endowees have been surprised and stunned by the experience may be seen in the carefully chosen remarks of Elder W. Grant Bangerter at the April, 1982 General Conference. "Having the privilege of working each day in the administration of the temples," said Elder Bangerter, swinging easily into temple-ese, "I am constantly impressed with the richness, the holiness, and the glory of the blessings administered there." And now the point: "Questions come to us about the ordinances performed in the temple." (What a world of anguish lies behind his affected innocence!) "We, of course, are not permitted," explains the faithful servant of God, "to discuss them outside the temple, because of their sacred nature." Apparently some members had complained at the sharp contradiction between what happens in the Endowment rooms and what they are led to expect. "Others press for a preparatory orientation so that those who enter the temple will not be confused." No chance, says Elder Bangerter, that we will give the dupes a break. "I want to emphasize that the preparation to enter the temple lies in the gospel. Nothing is said or done in the temple which does not have its foundation in the scriptures."

The truth is that not until one is in the Endowment Room of the temple, the doors closed and guarded, the spotters vigilantly watching every gesture, does the truth of total "consecration" on penalty of death come out. There is no aisle in the Endowment Room should one decide to run out; he would have to clamber over the bodies of the other experienced ritual throat-slitters, dodge past the spotters, and then race out of the building before anyone could react fast enough to stop him. Whether or not it would be more or less difficult to hitch a ride on the Capitol Beltway dressed in Temple robes is difficult to say. One would be considered either a lunatic and studiously ignored or a herald of the Second Coming and graciously assisted.

One Mormon publication describes an attempt to convert Hopi Indians to Mormonism:

> There are many Hopi beliefs that are close to LDS beliefs.... One of them told me: "I cannot join your church. I know it's true; I believe what it teaches, but I can't join it." I asked him to explain why.... "When we joined the Hopi religion, we made an oath that we would never depart from this religion."
>
> "What would happen to you if you departed from it?"

"Well, our lives would be taken."

He then made a motion of slitting his throat.

Hartman and Connie Rector, *No More Strangers*, (Bookcraft, 1971). In Mexico, there is a similar sect called the Pachuco's. "The only way you get out," I was told, "is in a pine box. It's not like the Mafia where they shoot you behind the ear: instead an accident takes place."

For a cult comparable to Mormonism within Anglo-Saxon culture, one need look no further than the organization that administers the following oath and penalty — and also dresses in white for its ceremonies:

> I, in the presence of Almighty God, do solemnly swear that I will never reveal to anyone not a member of the Order any of the Secrets, signs, passwords or mysteries of the Order. So help me God.

"Any member who shall reveal or betray the secrets of this Order," writes W.B. Romine in *The Story of the Original Ku Klux Klan*, "shall suffer the extreme penalty of the law."

The purpose of the endowment is to bind the soul of the victim irreversibly to the Mormon Church. The endowment is really a wedding ceremony, the wedding of the unsuspecting member to the hideous monster MORMO. There is no divorce from MORMO; for the disaffected there is only death. Today, unlike the muscular days of his youth, the monster is flabby and content with his national, indeed global success, and does not mind if a lot of his brides drift away. Few, however, dare tell the world about him — and reveal the awfulness of their wedding vows. I will let you go in peace, says MORMO, but woe unto him that tells my secrets. The endowment is actually the wedding supper of the devil; the main course is the soul of the bride. As one couple said in the August, 1974 *Ensign*: "Every time we return [to the temple], we are reminded of the covenants we have made, and this is the strongest motivation for us to continue the gospel way of life." The Church has established canneries around the country to fill its welfare storehouses. In a fictional representation of Mormon life in the nineteenth century, Gertrude Keene Major presents the following dialogue between two women working in one of these canneries:

LILA: Are you married?
HILDA: Yes, I've been canned in the temple.
LILA: Canned? You mean sealed.
HILDA: It's the same, sometimes the boss says seal the tomatoes, and sometimes he says can them.
LILA: It is just the same. It means that you can't get out.

Mormonism is an institution built on manipulation and intimidation. Joseph Smith is its Lenin; Sidney Rigdon its Trotsky; Brigham Young its Stalin and Spencer W. Kimball an aging Brezhnev. The power that founded it is evil, and the power that sustains it is death and the threat of death.

It is the kingdom of hell — and all who belong to it, despite its holy face, in the quiet of their captive souls instinctively know its hideousness. They just cannot see through it, and, therefore remain bound by its cunning. And then there are the few who love the thrill of power it provides, and would no more live without the fantasy than would a chain smoker without his cigarettes. Besides, who wants to admit that he has invested the best years of his life and his public reputation in an institution that can't pay off. It is a long drop for the soul from the celestial clouds of Mormon heaven to the concrete pavement of "they suckered me" reality — especially if one has raised a large family of children who, by dint of great effort, accepted the fantasy and initiated their children into it as well. Even more tragic — or farcical — is the situation of one who has named children after *Book of Mormon* heroes or married an Indian bride or husband because the *Book of Mormon* predicts a great future for them.

The unseen torture inflicted on the souls of thousands of victims of Mormonism who abhor its spirit but cannot psychologically free themselves from its power, the strange and anguished behavior that they exhibit in their inarticulate attempts to extricate themselves from bondage to the temple oaths, can only be adequately depicted by a Solzhenitsyn or an Orwell. If this book helps break the chains off the soul of one person who is suffocating in a Mormon life he despises but cannot fathom — if it leads one captive to freedom — then, gentlemen of the priesthood, my throat, my breast, and my bowels are yours.

Printed in the United States
216423BV00001B/84/A